ACCESS POLICY AND PROCEDURES AND THE LAW IN U.S. HIGHER EDUCATION

ACCESS TO HIGHER EDUCATION
AND THE LAW
Larry G. Simon

A REVIEW OF U.S. ADMISSIONS POLICIES
AND PRACTICES
Alice J. Irby

COLLEGE ADMISSIONS TESTING IN
THE UNITED STATES
Jenne K. Britell & William B. Schrader

NONINTELLECTUAL FACTORS IN ADMISSIONS
Simon V. Keochakian

CONTENTS

FOREWORD

In 1975 the International Council for Educational Development organized a comparative study of access policy and admissions practice with respect to higher education in the Federal Republic of Germany and the United States. This study, financed by a grant from the Volkswagen Foundation, was supervised by a joint German-U.S. Study Group, chaired by James A. Perkins, chairman of ICED, and directed by Barbara B. Burn, director of International Programs at the University of Massachusetts, Amherst. The final Study Group report was issued in mid-1978.

During the course of the study a number of special papers were commissioned and several conference reports were prepared. While all these documents made important contributions to the deliberations and final report, a few of them have such universal interest that it was decided to print them as part of the publication program of the access study.

Two major concerns of the Study Group were criteria and procedures for admission to higher education, and the relationship between higher education access and the law. In the volume—which treats the United States only—Larry Simon analyzes the role of law and especially the equal protection clause of the federal constitution on admissions, a topic made timely by the Bakke case. Alice Irby gives an overview of how admissions operates. College admissions testing in the United States, a subject of particular interest to Germany, is reviewed by Jenne Britell and William

Schrader. Simon Keochakian concentrates on nonintellectual factors in admissions. Amond them, these four essays thus provide a comprehensive discussion of the major aspects of admissions in the United States.

While the access study was basically a German-U.S. project, the problems examined are surely universal. For this reason it is hoped that this important document will be of interest and use to all those concerned with the pressing problem of providing an orderly and just system of access to higher education.

James A. Perkins
Chairman
International Council for
Educational Development

ACCESS TO
HIGHER EDUCATION
AND THE LAW

Larry G. Simon
University of Southern California

ACCESS TO
HIGHER EDUCATION
AND THE LAW

This essay was written to serve two purposes: first, to provice a concise if abbreviated introduction to the U.S. higher education system for West German scholars and officials participating in a binational study of higher education access policy; and second, to provide something of a ready reference of major institutional and legal considerations for American scholars and officials speculating about long-run U.S. higher education access policy. Its final three sections provide a general overview of the system of institutions, laws and legal principles within which the enterprise of higher education is conducted in the United States; its first longer section is a more detailed description of the major legal principles governing the admissions process. Because it was intended to provide a useful overview to different kinds of readers, some parts of it undoubtedly cover ground already familiar to many American nonlawyers, and attention to detail has often been sacrificed to its essential mapping and surveying aims.

I. Outline of the U.S. Governmental-Legal System

The United States Constitution is the fundamental legal instrument under which authority is allocated to government to make, administer, and apply law. The Constitution's three central features are: (1) the establishment of federalism; (2) the separation of powers of the federal (national) government among three branches; and (3) the creation of individual rights against government.

Federalism

The federal government is a government of limited powers or jurisdiction. Its power to make law is limited to the subjects specified in the Constitution. As to these subjects, federal law is supreme over state law, by virtue of the Constitution's Supremacy Clause. With regard to other subjects, the Tenth Amendment reserves to the states all governmental powers not conferred upon the federal government. Over the past 40 years or so, the federal government's law-making activities have greatly increased, under Supreme Court decisions expansively interpreting the Constitutional reach of federal power.

Separation of Powers

The Constitution divides the federal government into three branches. The legislative power, the authority to make law, is vested in Congress. The executive power, the authority to administer or enforce law, is vested in the President. The judicial power, the authority to interpret and apply law, is vested in the Supreme Court and "such inferior Courts as the Congress may from time to time ordain and establish." The Congress has created a federal judicial system, organized according to state-based geographical districts, consisting of trial courts (U.S. District Courts) and intermediate appellate courts (the U.S. Courts of Appeals), which hear appeals only on issues of law from the District Courts, and from which appeals (generally applications for discretionary review, called *certiorari*) may be taken to the U.S. Supreme Court.

As the activities of the federal government have increased, another institution has developed: the federal administrative agency. Dozens of agencies currently exercise regulatory powers over many features of the national life, and they typically perform mixtures of legislative, executive, and judicial functions. Administrative agencies are created by and their authority is specified by legislation enacted by Congress. When agencies first became common-place, the Supreme Court was much troubled by their constitutional legitimacy, and often held their creation entailed unlawful delegations by Congress of constitutionally nondelegable legislative powers. Those days have largely passed, and the agencies are now an accepted, familiar and important part of the federal government.

Rights Against Government

The U.S. Constitution contains several clauses which protect individual and private group rights against certain kinds of government action. Most of these provisions are in the Bill of Rights, the first ten amendments to the Constitution, and in the Fourteenth Amendment. The most important, as regards higher education, are the First and Fourteenth Amendments. The First Amendment, among other things, prohibits government from making any law "respecting an establishment of religion, or prohibiting the free exercise thereof; or abridging the freedom of speech." The Fourteenth Amendment provides that the government may not "deprive any person of life, liberty, or property, without due process of law; nor deny to any person within its jurisdiction the equal protection of the laws." These limitations have been held applicable, by Supreme Court decisions, to all branches of both state and federal government. Federal or state legislation, administrative regulation or any other form of government action which violates these provisions will be held "unconstitutional" by the courts, and may be enjoined or ordered remedied in other ways, including under some circumstances, awards of money damage judgments.

The States

By virtue of the Tenth Amendment, the 50 state governments possess all powers not prohibited them by the U.S. Constitution or federal law enacted by Congress under the

Constitution. The form and authority of government in each of the states depends upon the particular state's constitution. State constitutions, in the main, follow the separation of powers model of the U.S. Constitution, so that the state legislature makes law, the state executive (the governor) administers or enforces law, and the state judiciary (virtually always comprised of trial courts, intermediate appellate courts, and a supreme court) interpret and apply law. State courts also perform an additional role: they interpret and apply the common law, that unique institution of case by case judge-made law which we inherited from Great Britain.

Paralleling the federal developments, state administrative agencies have grown into an important part of state government. Again, these agencies commonly combine legislative, executive, and judicial functions, and their authority is specified by state legislation. Limitations upon the power of the legislature to delegate authority to agencies has retained considerably greater vitality in most states than it has at the federal level.

State constitutions also establish rights against the state, typically tracking the U.S. Constitution, but often going beyond. Roughly half the state constitutions also contain federalist-like provisions, allocating certain powers to agencies of local government, like city governments, rather than the state legislature.

II. The Governance of Higher Education

A. Federal Government

The U.S. Constitution does not expressly confer upon Congress the power to legislate in the area of education, and it has been assumed that education is one of the subjects reserved by the Tenth Amendment to the states. While Congress has not attempted any broad regulation of education, it has entered the field, primarily by conditioning the receipt of federal financial aid upon various nondiscrimination requirements, and the potential reach of more general federal power should not be underestimated. Probably Congress has substantial educational regulatory powers under its constitutional authority to enforce the provisions of the Fourteenth Amendment's due process and equal protection clauses. It probably also has substantial power to legislate or empower administrative agencies to make higher education policies under its constitutional authority to regulate activities affecting interstate commerce, a power liberally interpreted by the courts.

The constitutional basis of federal legislation which to date has most directly affected higher education has been Congress' power to "provide for the . . . general welfare." Though historically debated, the settled view now is that this "spending power" is an independent grant of authority and consequently expenditures need not be shown to come within some other grant of federal power, like the commerce clause. The only requirements are that the spending not violate some express constitutional prohibition, like that against Establishment of Religion, and that the spending be for the "general welfare" and the Courts will not reexamine Congress' determination of this latter issue. Moreover, the federal government can regulate behavior indirectly through the spending power, by setting conditions for the eligibility or receipt of aid, for example nondiscrimination on the basis of race. These conditions cannot lawfully violate other provisions of the Constitution, like the free speech clause, but have not so far proven amenable to attack on the basis of lack of federal power.

B. State Government

While Congress has asserted some regulatory jurisdiction over higher education and probably has considerable constitutional authority in the area, the states have been and remain the primary source of the law of higher education.

Although interstate variations make generalizations hazardous, we can identify the principal institutions and general legal principles under which they operate.

The cardinal prerequisite of legality in our system is that any action taken by any institution of government must be justifiable under the legal instruments that establish it and define its authority. The primary law-making institution of state government, the legislature, has been established by the state constitution, and any action taken by it must be supported expressly or by implication by the state constitution. The judiciary typically has the final word on this issue, subject to reversal only by constitutional amendment. The constitution of each of the states either itself establishes a state university or expressly or implicitly authorizes the legislature to establish one. The states' constitutions also either expressly or implicitly authorize the creation of private institutions of higher education, and the right to create such institutions may also be a federal constitutional right, as discussed later.

The distinction between the public and private sectors, in this as in other areas, has become increasingly blurred in recent years, though it still remains important in any assessment of legal rights and obligations. For present purposes it is sufficient to say that an institution of higher education is public if the state (or federal) government has been significantly involved in its establishment or operation; otherwise it is private. For some legal purposes this distinction is largely irrelevant. The federal and state governments have substantial constitutional authority to regulate the affairs of private institutions as well as public ones. Nonetheless, the public-private distinction can become legally significant, chiefly for two reasons: first, private institutions probably have certain constitutional protections against excessive governmental regulation not enjoyed by some public ones; second, the activity of private institutions, unlike public ones, is not subject to federal (or, normally, state) constitutional limitations, since these limitations apply only to "state action." There are today roughly 2,600 institutions of higher education in the United States, of which roughly 1,200 are public and 1,400 private, though more than two thirds of students attend public institutions. Approximately 700 of the public institutions are two-year colleges. About 800 of the private ones have some church affiliation. Postsecondary education as defined by many federal aid statutes also includes private profit and nonprofit trade and technical schools, public adult and area vocational schools, and various trade and union apprenticeship programs. There may be as many as 10,000 such institutions. And there are thousands of other "educational" enterprises like beauty and barber schools.

Public Institutions of Higher Education

Public institutions of higher education derive their authority either directly from the state constitution or from statutes enacted by the legislature. The question whether an institution is "constitutional" or "legislative" depends upon interpretation of constitutional language, and courts in different states have reached different results despite language similarities. For many purposes the distinction between constitutional and legislative institutions is unimportant. The actions of both count as state action for federal constitutional purposes, and both are equally and fully subject to pertinent federal statutory or administrative law. Both are subject to general state statutes enacted pursuant to the legislature's "police power," the power to pass laws of general applicability to promote the public health, safety or welfare (e.g. fire and safety standards, minimum wages, collective bargaining). Both are dependent on legislative appropriations, and to some extent subject to state restricted-use finance.

For some legal questions, however, the distinction can be important, though there are significant differences in the importance attached by the courts in different states. To overstate the distinction, a legislative institution is subject to the plenary power of the state legislature and is regarded by the courts more or less as any other administrative agency; whereas, a constitutional university is immune from some kinds of legislative or other state interference and is regarded by the courts more or less as a "fourth branch of government." Put in more realistic terms, a constitutional university is likely to have a wider range of judicially enforceable autonomy at least against attempts at relatively detailed management by legislatures or other administrative bodies, and perhaps to a limited extent against laws of general applicability which directly and substantially affect the educational mission of the university. Some protection is possible even against restricted use finance, that is, money grants made under regulatory conditions.[1]

Public institutions of higher education exist as state or local public corporations, as is most common, or as state administrative agencies. The distinction between a public corporation and a state agency tends often to be overexaggerated, though it may be important in a particular state. Historically, the courts have tended to be more generous with the former than the latter on issues involving the scope of judicial review of their actions and their implied powers, but the difference is one of degree and often the degree is small. The community colleges in many states are organized as geographical districts with local public corporate status. In other states they are state administrative agencies. Again, the difference between these forms of organization and between them and state public corporations will generally not be of great legal significance, though this depends on detailed state research and may involve issues relating to constitutional home rule provisions.

Whatever form of organization is employed, state constitutional or statutory law will provide for a system of governance for the state's public colleges and universities. The law will vest the control and management of the institution in a governing board, often called a board of trustees, and will specify the manner in which its members are to be selected. Selection systems differ from state to state but in the case of state institutions they usually involve participation by the governor, the legislature, or both. Members of a local institution's board are selected locally.

In some states, each geographically discrete campus offering higher education has its own governing board. The trend in recent years, however, has been away from individual institutional governance, though this centralization has taken different forms in different states. The range of interstate variation here is substantial. In the main, there have been three developments, which we may describe by the terms "state governing board," "multicampus governing board," and "state coordinating board." A state governing board has the authority to control and manage all of the state's public colleges and universities. A multicampus governing board has the authority to control several public institutions, though others may still have individual institutional governing boards. A state coordinating board has the authority to gather information and recommend long-range planning for the purpose of coordinating the activities of individual institutional and/or multicampus governing boards. Depending upon the state, the coordinating board may have some regulatory authority as well, though at some indeterminate degree of breadth and intensity of regulatory authority it becomes more accurate to view the coordinating board as a state governing board. Today, slightly more than 20 states have state governing boards. Most of the rest have coordinating boards, and roughly half of these exercise some regulatory powers. The precise governing arrangements within the states cannot be determined by relying upon the formal names of institutions, but require issue-oriented legal research.

Private Institutions of Higher Education

Private institutions of higher education are generally organized as nonprofit corporations, voluntary associations, or business corporations (if they are profit making). Such institutions are created and their authority defined by a charter, which must be filed and often approved by the state, though some of the older universities have been established by a special act of the state legislature or by state constitutional amendment. The U.S. Supreme Court in the early *Dartmouth College Case,*[2] held that a private university's charter is a contract, protected against subsequent state alteration by the Constitution's prohibition of state impairments of the obligations of contract. Subsequent case law has made quite clear, however, that the exceptions to this doctrine are sufficiently numerous that it affords very little practical protection to private institutions against state regulation, though it might still prevent a state "takeover."

Although the federal and state governments have substantial constitutional authority to regulate the affairs of private institutions of higher education, despite the contract clause, this power probably is limited at the extreme by certain constitutional doctrines which do not apply to public institutions. First, some extreme forms of government interference or regulation would probably be held by the courts to amount to takings of property subject to federal and state constitutional requirements obliging the state to pay just compensation. Second, many private colleges are church-related, and any state regulation which infringed religious freedoms would face constitutions. challenges under the free exercise of religion clause of the U.S. Constitution and similar clauses in state constitutions. Third, and of greatest potential general importance, it is possible that the right to choose private rather than public higher education (whether at a religious or nonsectarian institution) is itself a federal constitutional right. The U.S. Supreme Court, more than 50 years ago, held in a case involving state preclusion of private elementary education that a parent's right to control the upbringing of his children was a "liberty" protected against "unreasonable" state interference of this sort by the due process clause of the Fourteenth Amendment.[3] Related decisions held that, at some level of intensity, state regulation of private elementary and secondary schools impermissibly infringes this liberty.[4] After these decisions, their "natural law" approach fell into disrepute for three decades, but it has recently been revived by the Court. Some Justices and legal scholars interpret the private school right, retrospectively, as a free speech-derivative right, and if faced with an appropriate higher education case, the Court might well adopt this view. If so, this would presumably preclude some extreme forms of state regulation of private institutions.

Whatever the constitutional scope of state power over private institutions, neither the federal government nor the states have chosen to regulate their academic affairs extensively, though again there are interstate variations and a trend toward subjecting private institutions to the noncoercive authority of state higher education coordinating boards. In general, though, the form of governance of a private institution depends on the terms of its charter, and typically the charter vests control and management in a governing board, generally called a board of trustees. Historically, most charters provided that governing boards would select their own replacement members, but many private institutions have secured amendments to their charters providing for the election of at least some governing board members by alumni and sometimes by other interested groups.

Internal Governance

Although in legal theory the governing board of a private or public university is that university's government, subject, of course, to any applicable federal or state constitutional or statutory requirements, governing boards have in fact delegated many of their powers to the president of the institution or to other administrative officers, or the faculties, departments, students, or other groups.

Often the governing board is authorized by statute or charter to delegate its powers, but sometimes there is no such express authorization. In these instances, the president or someone else who exercises a delegated power may be vulnerable to legal challenge, though there have not been many cases litigating this question. In any event, in the absence of exceptional legislation (or intervening constitutional claims) the governing board cannot make irrevocable delegations of powers vested in it by statute or charter. That is, in general it retains the legal authority to countermand decisions or, of course, to rescind the delegation. Irrevocable reallocations of decision-making power may require state constitutional amendments as regards constitutional universities. For legislative institutions, legislative reform would be necessary, and for private institutions, normally a charter amendment (which is virtually always possible when the current governing board consents).

Accrediting Agencies

Agencies external to the individual institutions of higher education set minimal program and general quality standards for accreditation. In some states, accreditation may be a legal prerequisite to an institution's operation, but in any event institutions have great incentives to comply with accreditation standards. Their attractiveness to students depends partially on accreditation, as does their eligibility for federal and sometimes state aid. The three main types of accrediting agencies are: state agencies that set educational standards prerequisite to licensing for various occupations; private regional associations that set standards for general education programs; and national professional and vocational associations that set occupational entrance standards.

III. Financing Higher Education

Institutions of higher education derive their revenues from many sources: tuition and other fees; state taxation, and in the case of community colleges, local taxation as well; endowment funds and annual donations and gifts; a variety of revenue raising activities, like ticket fees for sports events; and, of ever-increasing importance, federal taxation.

State Finance of Public Institutions

State constitutions rarely contain provisions bearing uniquely on legislative power to tax and spend for higher education, though of course all general constitutional provisions bearing on finance—prohibiting certain forms of taxation, or specifying the appropriation process, for example—are normally applicable to higher education finance. The major tax sources for most states are sales and state income. In general, legislatures have great discretion to set the level of funding and control the purposes for which funds can be spent. Community colleges also rely on local property taxation, and are often subject at the local level to a budgetary process similar to the state process here outlined.

The budget-making process supposedly begins within individual departments or schools of individual institutions or campuses. From this point, the budget passes through ever-centralizing review and consolidation into a uniform budget for higher education, often passing through a state coordinating board for at least recommendations, to a state level budget office, typically subject to the governor's control. It is then reviewed by legislative committees and thereafter is voted upon by legislature. The budget passed by the legislature (for which it will then appropriate funds) is legally an expenditure control instrument, and institutions cannot deviate from its specifications, except as authorized by law.

In recent years, state executives and legislatures have increasingly used their budget powers to influence or control institutions of higher education. Partly this has been because of financial pressures, partly because of unhappiness over "campus unrest," and partly because the increasing sophistication in technology and the social sciences has provided techniques for management, control, and spurred a quest for "educational efficiency." A variety of budget-control techniques have been employed, for example, conditions attached to line-item appropriations, riders on the appropriation bill to specify certain uses for funds, negotiated agreements between governors' offices and institutions. In addition, of course, the shift toward program planning and budgeting systems entails greater centralization of policy.

Legislative universities have virtually no general legal recourse against external budget control. Court decisions confirm that constitutional universities have some protections, at least against the more egregious forms of control, though again there are interstate differences and constitutional universities are by no means completely protected. Some decisions suggest, for example, that some control through conditional grants is permissible, and it is rather difficult to see how courts might limit politically expedient negotiated agreements.

State Aid to Private Institutions

At least 36 states now provide some form of public aid to private institutions, though this accounts for a very small percentage of private revenue. In most of these states, the aid is in the form of scholarships, loans or tuition grants for state residents, and often is available only for attendance at institutions within the state. There are some constitutional limitations on the extent to which public tuition aid can be granted to sectarian institutions, as we shall discuss later. Private nonprofit institutions are granted exemptions from state and local taxes in virtually all states. Several states also provide an indirect capital subsidy to private institutions by, in effect, issuing public bonds on their behalf. This form of indirect subsidy, as well as any other form of aid to private institutions, can run into problems under varying though common state constitutional provisions prohibiting public aid to private organizations. The courts tend, however, to approve tuition aid on the theory that it is for the student, not the institution, and revenue bonds on the theory that they do not pledge tax funds. But indirect institutional grants would be legally problematic in many states.

Tuition

Some state constitutions bar public institutions from charging tuition. It is reasonably clear, though, that there is no federal constitutional prohibition on public tuition. The U.S. Supreme Court has held that the states may not deny indigents certain fundamental rights for lack of a fee payment. But recent cases demonstrate the Court is narrowly confining this principle, and it recently held that even elementary and secondary education is not a fundamental right.[5] This is a sporadically dynamic area of constitutional law, however, and a plausible argument could be made distinguishing the precedents, especially under unlikely extreme circumstances, as if no loan money were available.[6]

Private tuition levels are about four times higher than public ones. Private institutions set their own tuition rates, disciplined by market forces but not law, and there is some case law suggesting that private tuitions may be beyond state regulatory power, except in extraordinary situations. In addition to the various state and federal tuition aids, many private institutions use gift or endowment funds to help needy students, and philanthropic organizations also provide some assistance.

The governing boards of public legislative institutions apparently have discretion in setting tuition, but must comply with any constitutional or legislative restrictions. As a practical matter, though, the budgetary process must itself affect this discretion, since, for example, a foreseeable underappropriation of tax revenues may leave no choice but a tuition increase. Although in theory constitutional governing boards sometimes appear to have autonomy in setting tuition and controlling tuition revenues, it is difficult to understand why, as a matter of practical politics, the same basic forces would not operate in the long run.

Higher Tuition for Nonresidents

States often levy higher public tuition rates upon students who are not state residents. The U.S. Supreme Court in *Vlandis* v. *Kline*[7] ruled unconstitutional a state statute denying students resident tuition for their entire college career when, if married, their legal address was out-of-state at the time of application, or, if single, it was out-of-state at any time during the year preceding application. According to the Court, this "irrebuttable presumption" of nonresidence (i.e. an intent not to permanently reside in the state) denied students due process of law by foreclosing their opportunity to submit evidence showing that they were in fact state residents. At a minimum, this case prohibits the conclusive assumption that a student coming from out-of-state will remain a nonresident for his entire time in college. Its implication for common durational residency requirements is less clear, since the Court at the time recognized the state's interest in maintaining tuition

preferences for "bona fide residents." Complicating the
question further, the Court has on several occasions affirmed without opinion lower court decisions upholding
durational residency requirements for instate tuition, and
very recently has somewhat ambiguously suggested that
the question whether or not a student is a state resident (or
domiciliary) for tuition purposes is solely a question of
state law.[8] If this latter proposition were true, the *Vlandis*
case would be of greatly diminished importance: The states
might remain constitutionally barred from conclusively assuming that students within a certain category would never
have the requisite intent of permanent residence such that
they could become residents, but the states could instead
redefine the concept of "residency" so as, for example, to
include characteristics like "x years actual living within the
state," to accomplish the same goal.

The extent of state power to define residency and/or
discriminate between state residents and nonresidents is
obviously not clear. In order to resolve the issue, the courts
must cease engaging in whimsical pursuits of a general legal
concept of residency and focus instead on the competing
interests at stake. State tuition disfavoritism of nonresidents (or recent arrivals) is normally based on an attempt
to approximate some rough equalization between past or
predicted future tax contributions and education costs.
This interest is certainly significant enough to justify the
state in disfavoring daily commuter students who each
morning enter the state to attend classes and each evening
return to their homes in other states. Equally certainly, the
tax-cost equalization interest is not significant enough to
justify disfavorable treatment for all students except those
who were born and have continuously lived in the state.
The question is where to draw the line, and quite probably
the courts will in the end permit durational residency
requirements in the neighborhood of one year, but become increasingly skeptical of longer requirements. In some

circumstances, moreover, the state's tax-cost equalization interest may be given even less weight. Thus, for example, disfavorable treatment of certain classes of aliens who are exempt from state taxes by virtue of U.S. treaty obligations may ultimately be held unconstitutional under the Supremacy Clause, as unwarranted intrusions upon federal interests.[9]

Interstate Compacts

Some states have entered into regional educational compacts, in part to cope with interstate student migration and related tuition problems. The boards created by such compacts sometimes arrange for interstate placements of graduate and professional students and make required financial adjustments. States have often proceeded on the assumption that such compacts require Congressional approval by virtue of the Constitutional clause on interstate agreements, but Supreme Court decisions suggest that this assumption is incorrect.

Federal Funds

As noted earlier, Congress has great constitutional freedom to spend and to attach conditions to the receipt of federal funds, so long as it transgresses no express constitutional prohibition, most prominently the Establishment of Religion Clause, discussed later. Federal tax-raised funds flow to higher education under dozens of statutes, and programs, formulae and arrangements. Some programs send funds directly to institutions; some to students; some to faculty, either for study or research. Some funds are for general and others for restricted uses. Most subsidize operating costs, but some are for capital expenditures. Some are disbursed under statutory formulae, and others through administrative discretion. Some flow as direct grants, but others are loans or loan subsidies.

The major student assistance programs were established by the Veterans' Readjustment Benefits Act of 1966, as amended, 1976;[10] the Social Security Act of 1935, as amended 1974;[11] and the Higher Education Act of 1965, as amended 1977.[12] Under the first statute, veterans are eligible for monthly stipends, if attending a secondary or postsecondary education institution. A major change was made by the 1976 amendments: Education assistance for those entering the armed forces after December 1, 1976 is provided only if the person elects to participate in the program by having a monthly deduction taken from his or her pay.

Under the Social Security Act, any child up to the age of 22 may receive payments for attending many kinds of educational institutions (including higher education), if either of the child's parents has died, become disabled, or retired while covered by the Social Security program. In order to qualify, the child must be unmarried and a full-time student.

The Higher Education Act, under the general supervision of the U.S. Commissioner of Education, provides for several student assistance programs. In general, these programs support students in undergraduate institutions, two-year institutions, shorter term programs aimed at gainful employment, and nursing schools, whether public, private, nonprofit, or proprietary. Graduate students may qualify for some of the loan programs. To be eligible for these, as for other federal programs, an institution must generally be accredited by an accrediting agency on a list of more than 60 maintained by the commissioner. Most of the programs are directed at financially needy students.

Basic Educational Opportunity Grants are authorized for up to $1,800 per student per year, minus expected family contributions as computed under a specified formula, but may not exceed half of actual attendance costs or total costs minus expected family contributions. Awards of under $200 will not be made, and a reduction scale specifies adjustments for years when appropriations are below the authorization level. Supplemental Educational Opportunity Grants are available for students from poor families with exceptional need and signs of academic or creative promise. Funds for these grants are provided to institutions with special agreements with the commissioner; the institutions then award eligible students up to $1,500 or half of the financial aid provided the student by the institution, whichever is less. Direct student loans are available for students who need financial assistance, through federal funds made available through agreements executed between the commissioner and the participating institution, which must itself contribute one ninth of the federal contribution and conform to other fiscal requirements. The federal government also insures loans, up to a maximum interest rate, obtained by students from private lending institutions, regardless of their financial need. Students from families with incomes below $25,000 (and in some cases, above $25,000) qualify for interest-subsidized insured loans. Federal work-study grants are available for students with financial need, to subsidize their part-time employment by the participating institution or a public or nonprofit corporation. Funds under this program are allotted to states, under a formula reflecting high school graduates, full-time higher education enrollments, and concentrations of poor people. The federal share cannot exceed 80 percent of costs, unless the institution serves students predominantly from low-income families. Finally, the federal government provides incentive grants to states on a 50-50 matching basis which make grants to students with substantial financial need, as defined by the commissioner.

A great many other federal programs send money to higher education. Grants and loans are available under several statutes for construction and equipment purchase.

Many courses of study, especially but not limited to science and health, are subsidized. Merit scholarships are available for teachers and other occupations. And finally, of course, billions of dollars are spent each year by many federal agencies, like the National Science Foundation, to subsidize or purchase particular research.

Note should be taken of the importance of federal tax as well as spending policy. Most importantly, public and nonprofit institutions are basically exempt from federal income taxation. Private donors to such institutions can deduct donations from their taxable income. The interest on state and local bonds used to finance higher education construction is also income-tax exempt, substantially reducing the cost of borrowing.

Establishment of Religion

Neither state nor federal aid to private institutions may violate the ban on Establishments of Religion of the First Amendment. In order to survive Establishment challenge, a law must have a secular purpose, a primarily secular effect, and must not entangle church and state by an excessive regulatory scheme. The Court has been extremely restrictive in the elementary-secondary school area, even striking down tuition subsidies and tax benefits for the students or their parents. It has been more lenient regarding higher education (on the general basis that college students are at a less impressionable age), allowing a nonreligious earmarked federal construction aid program and similar state indirect capital aid through revenue bond finance.[13] In a 1976 opinion the Supreme Court considered the constitutionality of a Maryland statute which provided for annual noncategorical grants to private colleges (among them religiously affiliated institutions) with only one restriction, that the funds not be used for "sectarian purposes."[14] The

Court examined the role of religion on the campuses of the four religiously affiliated Maryland institutions and upheld the District Court's finding that these colleges were not "pervasively sectarian." In evaluating the role of religion in these colleges, the Supreme Court examined each institution individually to determine whether it was highly or minimally sectarian, taking account of factors like its governance and financial relations with the church, its religious admissions policy, its requirements regarding devotional exercises and its curriculum, and the degree of academic freedom given the faculty.

The Supreme Court recently affirmed without opinion two lower courts' opinions which dealt with the question of tuition subsidies to needy students.[15] The challenged Tennessee statute provided grants directly to students to be spent only on educationally related expenses, including tuition (the district court likened it to the G.I. Bill) at the accredited Tennessee college of their choice. The Tennessee District Court held that by providing grants directly to students "[n]o one religion is favored by the program, nor are religious institutions favored over public institutions." In addition to direct grants to students, the challenged North Carolina scheme of free scholarship and tuition assistance provided funds to institutions so that the institutions can give a $200 credit on tuition bills to qualified students. The court compared the role of religion in the colleges involved in the case to the four colleges involved in the previously mentioned case and found that these colleges too were not pervasively sectarian.

Notwithstanding this relatively permissible posture on federal constitutional law, there is still considerable pressure on religiously affiliated institutions to abandon any church relationship, by seeking charter amendments, as many have already done. This movement seems likely to continue because a majority of the states have constitutional provisions precluding aid to religious institutions, which are often more restrictive than the First Amendment of the United States Constitution.

IV. Admission to Institutions of Higher Education

The accessibility of different institutions of higher education to different students obviously depends enormously upon tuition levels, the levels of federal, state, and local tax support and the types of public and private tuition subsidies. Today there are enough public institutions charging no or low tuition, and sufficient loan and grant subsidies available so that most high school graduates who wish to go on to higher education can probably do so. It does not follow, however, that anyone can attend any institution. Even apart from unsubsidized (though often deferrable) cost differences, the individual must first be admitted by the institution; that is, he or she must satisfy whatever criteria the institution establishes as prerequisite to attendance. The following discussion of admissions is organized into three sections: authority over admissions; criteria of admissions; and admissions processes.[16]

A. Authority over Admissions

State constitutions and legislation rarely set detailed policies to govern the admissions process, though statutes in some states do provide that all high school graduates above a certain grade rank are entitled or eligible for admission to certain public institutions, or that public two-year colleges shall be open to all high school graduates. More commonly, state law, like federal law, prohibits the employment of certain admission criteria and otherwise expressly or implicitly delegates to governing boards power over the admissions process. Private governing boards derive this power from their charters, and occasionally from legislation as well.

There is little question that legislatures have constitutional authority to intrude more directly upon admissions policies of legislative institutions. Legislative authority over admissions to constitutional universities is probably more limited, though there appear to be few cases on point and the particulars of constitutional autonomy depend upon the case law as developed in each state. State legislatures also have considerable power to regulate the admissions policies of private institutions, though there are obviously special obstacles to intruding into the selection of students by religious institutions. More generally, if a state wished to employ a form of regulation which substantially damaged a private institution financially, it might be required to pay just compensation. And at some level of intrusiveness state regulation of admissions might well trench on private choice values protected by the U.S. Constitution, and, at the least, require a strong justification to withstand challenge.

Ultimate questions of legislative power aside, the principle vulnerability to legal challenge on general "lack of authority" grounds of the typical legislative institution admissions systems arises because state statutes often confer discretion to governing boards to make admissions policies. Although actual legal challenges to these delegations have been rare, they could be challenged on the ground that in failing to provide any standards for admissions, the legislature has transferred its power to a nonlegislature. Under some circumstances, internal redelegations could conceivably also give rise to plausible challenges, though "ministerial" tasks can normally be delegated without restriction and real problems are likely only where the delegation is arguably inconsistent with legislation.

State coordinating boards appear very rarely to have any direct authority over the student selection standards of institutions, though they sometimes have powers which indirectly affect admissions, like setting standards for the granting of degrees. The question of ultimate state legislative power to expand the admissions regulation of state coordinating boards is not materially different from legislative power to legislate admissions standards directly: as to legislative universities, the state legislature's power is extensive; whereas, constitutional and private institutions have some outside protections. An open-ended legislative delegation of admissions policy power to a coordinating board could also be subject to the same form of delegation challenge as noted with regard to legislative governing boards. In the absence of express legislation, the scope of a coordinating board's authority over admissions depends upon interpretation of the relevant legislation.

Finally, state legislation sometimes affects admissions quite directly by requiring institutions to comply with standards set by private or public accrediting agencies, and these often include admissions-related standards. State legislation may also require state agency accreditation, which may include some admissions standards, as prerequisite for graduates of a professional or occupational school obtaining licensing or certification. Of at least equal importance, accreditation is a prerequisite to participation in many federal aid programs, and while such federal regulation is noncoercive it obviously creates great incentives for compliance. In general, analysis of the legislature's ultimate power to establish (or disestablish) accreditation requirements affecting admissions is similar to its power to set standards directly, as discussed previously, although the precise form of legislation and sanctions for noncompliance could be legally relevant. For example, legislation establishing graduation from an accredited institution as prerequisite for professional or occupational licensing would probably stand on firmer grounds, insofar as challenges by constitutional universities are concerned, than legislation making accreditation prerequisite to their operation, since the former is more easily defensible as an exercise of the legislature's general police power. Special delegation problems may also arise if legislation requires compliance with all future

modifications of the accreditation standards of a private
accreditation agency, but otherwise the delegation issues
do not differ significantly from those previously discussed.

B. Criteria of Admissions

Subject to the standard cautions about interstate variation, then, admissions policies are "normally" set by governing boards. Whether operating in this normal manner or
under more mandatory legislative schemes, institutions of
higher education in the United States have either academically "selective" or "open" admissions policies.

Selective and Open Admissions Policies

An institution with a selective policy admits students on
the basis of predictions as to how well they will perform in
higher education. These predictions are based primarily
upon students' grades in secondary school and/or scores on
the Scholastic Aptitude Test (SAT). By contrast, an institution with an open admissions policy accepts all students
who apply, except perhaps those who are incapable of
benefiting from the institution's educational program. Most
private and public four-year colleges and universities have
selective admissions policies, though the type and degree
of selectivity depends upon policy choices of the institution and upon its competitive attractiveness to top calibre
students. Some may admit only students in the top 5 percent of their high school class and SAT; others in the top
20, or 50 percent, with or without regard to SAT, and so
on. State or multicampus governing boards may set different standards for different public institutions. Virtually all
public two-year and many public four-year colleges have
open admissions policies, and the student bodies of the
two-year institutions are generally comprised of those who
were in the bottom third of their high school class.

In addition to academic selection criteria, institutions of
higher education have historically employed nonacademic

criteria, whether of their own choice or pursuant to mandatory legislation. These nonacademic criteria have been the chief source of legal problems.

The Equal Protection Clause in General

The most important legal limitation upon admissions criteria is the Equal Protection Clause of the Fourteenth Amendment to the U.S. Constitution. Over the past 20 years or so, the courts have used a two-tiered approach in adjudicating equal protection challenges. When the state treats classes of individuals differently, its classification must normally be shown to be rationally related to a permissible state purpose or goal. Historically, this rationality test was generally applied in cases challenging state economic or welfare policies, and virtually always resulted in a rejection of the challenge, since minimal rationality is easy to establish. On the other hand, when the state treats individuals differently on the basis of race or some other "suspect" classification, such differential treatment will be held unconstitutional unless shown to promote some "compelling state interest" which could not be reasonably well promoted through alternative means. Very rarely will such a showing be possible.

From time to time, the Supreme Court has also used this second approach in adjudicating challenges to classifications affecting what are sometimes called "fundamental interests." In 1973, however, the Court held that elementary and secondary education was not a fundamental interest for federal constitutional purposes, and it follows, almost certainly, that higher education is not one either.[17] In any event, the present Supreme Court has at least partially repudiated this fundamental interest branch of equal protection. At the same time, however, the present Court has given signs, often ambiguously, of strengthening the requirements of the traditional rationality test, so that in the

future it is possible that many forms of differential treatment will be subject to a somewhat higher burden of justification (though not the compelling interest test), even
though they do not entail suspect classifications. The clear-
est manifestation of this intermediate burden of justification is in the still-emerging area of sex (gender) discrimination, where the Court has recently indicated that sex classification must be shown to substantially further important
governmental interests.[18]

The equal protection clause limits discrimination by the
state only. Sometimes, however, the activities of allegedly
private institutions are regarded as "state action" for constitutional purposes. This state action problem has rightly
been called the most important problem in American Constitutional Law, and it is far from solved. Currently, the
question is determined on a case by case basis, with the
courts employing a variety of sometimes shifting tests. The
fact that the institution's charter is state-approved or that
it is slightly regulated by the state, or exempt from state
taxation, will *not* independently or, probably, in combination result in a finding of state action. Neither will the fact
that the institution receives state or federal financial aid.
Direct state involvement in management, for example, in
appointing its board of governors, would likely result in a
finding of state action. Also, if the state intensively regu-
lates a feature of the institution's behavior, such that the
state can be characterized as putting its *imprimatur* upon
the private action, that particular feature might well be regarded as state action.[19] Perhaps the behavior of an institution which could not operate but for public aid might also
qualify, though this remains an open question. A state action finding may also be based on various combinations
and permutations of the above criteria. It seems fairly clear
however, that despite some hints over the years, the Supreme Court is not prepared to hold that all institutions of
higher educations are, in effect, arms of the government,

on the theory that education is an "inherently public function."

Racial Discrimination and Racially Preferential Admissions

The equal protection clause, then, applies to legislative and constitutional institutions of higher education, and to those activities of private institutions that count as state action. With regard to admissions policies and practices, the clause clearly prohibits discrimination against members of minority racial groups. The ban on racial discrimination extends not only to racial prerequisites for admission, but also to criteria which may be apparently neutral but which were adopted for the purpose and have the effect of achieving this racially discriminatory goal. Partly because racial motivation is generally absent and partly because it is difficult to prove, this ban on discriminatorily motivated admissions policies is of limited practical importance.

The more important question, indeed one of the most important questions relating to admissions to higher education, is whether and to what extent proof of a disparate racial impact alone can establish a constitutional violation. This general issue (though not in higher education) has been in and out of courts very often in the past decade, and was recently settled (at least for the time being) by a decision of the U.S. Supreme Court.

The recent important developments in this area have their roots not in constitutional law as such, but in regulations developed by the U.S. Equal Employment Opportunity Commission (EEOC) under Title VII (employment discrimination) of the Civil Rights Act of 1964.[20] EEOC regulations prohibit the use of employment tests or job qualifications (like high school diplomas) which have the effect of rejecting minority groups protected by the Act at a higher rate than whites, unless the employer sustains the burden of proving that the test accurately predicts important attributes of job performance. The Supreme Court sustained these EEOC regulations, and soon thereafter the lower courts began to hold that the equal protection clause of its own force made the same standards applicable to state action. Lower Federal courts in California, for example, applied this analysis to hold that elementary schools cannot use IQ tests as the basis for assigning black children to "educable mentally retarded" classes.

The U.S. Supreme Court recently rejected this interpretation of the Equal Protection Clause, in the course repudiating several lower court decisions.[21] The Court held that the fact that the effect of a government action is to relative disadvantage members of a racial group is not constitutionally significant. In order to make out an equal protection violation, a plaintiff must prove that the action was discriminatorily motivated. Thus, the plaintiff in the case before the Court was unsuccessful in challenging the constitutionality of a civil service test, the effect of which was to disqualify black applicants at four times the rate of whites. This racially disproportionate effect itself was not presumptively unconstitutional and the plaintiff had failed to prove that the test was adopted or used for the goal of discriminating against blacks. By a parity of reasoning, it seems clear that university admission criteria are not unconstitutional simply because they relatively disadvantage blacks or some other racial group.

Partly in recognition of the fact that uniform application of admission criteria would significantly disadvantage blacks and other racial minority groups, many selective institutions have in the last few years adopted admissions systems which grant preference to such minorities. This is currently a major issue in Equal Protection Law. The general issue is the constitutionality of "reverse discrimination" or "benevolent quotas," a practice which, as it arises in higher education admissions, typically involves separating minority and majority applicants into two applicant pools, and judging the applicants in each pool competitively with others in the same pool but not with those in the other. The outcome is that selective institutions admit minority students whose prior grades and standardized test scores are often considerably lower than majority group applicants who are rejected. Sometimes, minority students are admitted on this basis up to some fixed percentage (quota) of the entering class, and sometimes, so it is claimed, on some other basis.

Lower courts have reached differing results on this issue, and it will soon be resolved by the Supreme Court. Several terms ago, the Court heard argument in one such case, *DeFunis* v *Odegaard*,[22] but dismissed it as moot without reaching the constitutional question. The question is now pending before the Supreme Court in *California Board of Regents* v. *Bakke*.[23] The legal literature is replete with analyses, suggesting a variety of approaches. Very briefly, the major arguments against the constitutionality of preferential admissions fall into two groups: that race is *per se* a constitutionally impermissible classifying trait; and that even if not, it is impermissible as employed in preferential admissions. The first argument rests on the claim that the "Constitution is colorblind," and has never been accepted by the Supreme Court. Instead, prevailing doctrine holds that racial classifications are suspect, but can be upheld if shown necessary to promote a compelling state interest. Arguments in the second group take different forms. Sometimes they rest on distinctions, which seem artificial, between quotas and other systems. At other times, their gist is that there is no compelling state interest here which could not be satisfied a better way. Arguments for constitutionality typically claim that the state's interest in redressing past discrimination, integrating institutions, providing more minority professionals and the like are compelling, and, when the importance of producing social change quickly is taken into account, can be accomplished only this way. Others in this camp have taken differing tacks, arguing, for example, that the ban on racial discrimination applies only to "hostile" discrimination or racially prejudiced government action, and that prejudice against whites played no role in the adoption of preferences for minority groups.

The preferential admissions issue is connected to the previously mentioned (but now settled) dispute concerning the constitutional significance of government actions which produce racially disproportionate effects. As noted previously, the uniform application of admissions criteria would not be unconstitutional even if it seriously disadvantaged blacks and similarly situated groups. Thus, racially preferential policies are clearly not constitutionally *required.* The pending *Bakke* case raises the question whether such policies are constitutionally *permissible,* and if the Court holds that they are not, the question whether and to what extent public universities will remain free to specially help minority groups through means other than overt racial preferences depends very much on the exact rationale of the Court's assumed decision. Whether, for example, a general preferential admission program for the economically disadvantaged would survive constitutional attack cannot be confidently predicted at this time. The mere fact that such a program advantaged blacks relative to whites would not make it unconstitutional, for as we have seen, racially disproportionate effect alone does not establish a constitutional violation. On the other hand, we have also seen that an equal protection violation is established if the plaintiff proves racially discriminatory motivation. Suppose, then, that a white plaintiff proved that a preferential admissions program for the economically disadvantaged was in substantial part motivated by a desire to help blacks? It is by no means clear that the problem can be solved simply by distinguishing between "prejudiced" and "benign" racial motivation, for this same distinction would suggest, contrary to our present assumption, that overtly racial preferences of the sort at issue in *Bakke* are themselves constitutionally inoffensive. Thus, predictions of the constitutionality of programs like our assumed preference for the disadvantaged must await the Court's decision in *Bakke*.

Statutory Regulation of Racial and Similar Discrimination

Although recent federal legislation does not prohibit racial discrimination by private institutions of higher education, the lower federal courts have recently reinterpreted a provision of the 1868 Civil Rights Act to prohibit such discrimination. Moreover, state legislation in many states outlaws such discrimination, and the common law of private association is also moving in this direction. In addition private schools which racially discriminate are likely to lose their tax-exempt status.[23a] Finally, federal legislation provides that:

> No person in the United States shall, on the ground of race, color, or national origin, be excluded from participating in, be denied the benefits of, or be subjected to discrimination under any program or activity receiving Federal financial assistance.[24]

Under this provision, no discriminating institution of higher education, public or private, may receive federal funds.[24a] The provision is unquestionably within Congress' constitutional power to condition the expenditure of federal funds. It is administered by the Department of Health, Education, and Welfare (HEW), which has promulgated regulations making more particular the requirements. These regulations, among other matters, require institutions that previously discriminated to take "affirmative action" to overcome the effects of such discrimination. With respect

to most institutions—those which did not previously discriminate—the regulations permit but do not require affirmative action. Thus, preferential admissions policies do
not currently jeopardize an institution's federal aid, but
the constitutionality of these HEW regulations depends on
the Supreme Court's resolution of the *Bakke* and related
issues. If the Supreme Court were to hold that racially preferential admissions programs are unconstitutional, it would
also violate the above quoted federal statute. While the
constitutional prohibition would apply only to public institutions, therefore, private institutions could continue
preferential programs only at the risk of losing federal
financial assistance.

Note should also be taken of the EEOC employment
discrimination regulations mentioned previously. These apply to institutions of higher education in their employer
capacities. More pertinent to access policy, however, the
EEOC regulations on credentials and tests prerequisite to
employment may, in the long run, have an enormous impact on access to higher education. For example: If a substantial line of cases develop holding that high school diplomas and other types of credentials (and degrees?) cannot legally be required of any minority applicants for many
types of jobs, the pattern of demand for education of all
types and at all levels may well be affected.

Sex Discrimination

Over the past several years, there has been a continuing
and not completely resolved debate among the Justices of
the U.S. Supreme Court on the question whether sex, like
race, is a suspect classification. Currently, sex classifications are not suspect, but nonetheless must surpass a higher
burden of justification than the "mere rationality" standard. In *Craig* v. *Boren,* decided in 1976, the Court held that
sex classifications are unconstitutional unless they "serve

important governmental objectives and . . . [are] substantially related to achievement of those objectives.[25] Although the Court has not subsequently always applied this standard, it has been extremely reluctant to uphold any challenged sex classification. Putting aside the special problem posed by single-sex institutions, it seems unlikely that any sex-related admissions criteria which operated to disadvantage women could withstand constitutional attack. To justify such an admissions criterion, a university would have to establish that it was not a consequence of sexual stereotyping, that its goal was an extremely important one, and that the sex classification was an eminently sensible way to accomplish this important goal. It is simply hard to imagine that these showings could be made with respect to sex-based admissions criteria.

The two issue areas in which more difficult constitutional sex discrimination problems can arise with respect to university admissions involve single-sex institutions and benign discrimination in favor of women. Several lower courts have upheld the constitutionality of single-sex institutions, so long as they do not prevent unique general quality or specific training opportunities not otherwise available to the excluded sex: that is, "separate but equal" facilities have thus far passed constitutional muster. It is extremely difficult to predict how the Supreme Court will respond to this issue if and when it is squarely presented, because constitutional sex discrimination cases decided to date have not involved sexual segregation.[26] Assuming that the Supreme Court were inclined to uphold single-sex institutions, the most that can be predicted with some confidence is that the Court would probably adopt the separate but equal approach of the lower courts. Thus, for example, a campus in a state university or college system might be able to constitute itself a men's school, so long as the same type and quality of education was otherwise available within the state system for women.

With regard to benign discrimination favoring women in the admissions process, the Supreme Court has on several occasions upheld such benign sex classifications, but has looked closely to assure itself that the classification was truly benign. Thus, for example, an institution which had previously been open to men only, but which determined to become co-educational, could probably grant preferential admissions treatment to women in order to expedite the transition. Similarly, a graduate or professional school in a discipline from which women have been historically excluded or in which they are currently seriously under-represented could probably initiate such sexual preferences. We should emphasize, however, that the law in this area is really quite unclear, and the foregoing propositions are little more than informed speculation. Perhaps, the Supreme Court's awaited decision in the *Bakke* case will shed some light on this comparable issue in sex discrimination.

While some states have statutory prohibitions against sex discrimination, the principal statutory scheme is the federal ban against sex discrimination in certain education programs receiving federal assistance, enacted in the education amendments of 1972.[27] This statute applies to the admissions process of many public and private institutions of higher education, but there are some important exceptions: private undergraduate schools that have had a continuous tradition of single-sex admissions; private church-related schools whose tenets preclude admission of both sexes; and military training schools. Institutions covered by the statute—most public undergraduate and the vast majority of public and private graduate, professional and vocational schools—can have their federal funds terminated for discrimination in admissions, and in certain circumstances are liable to injunctive suit by the federal government.

Citizenship and Residency Discrimination

The Supreme Court has held that resident alienage is a suspect classification, and has struck down almost all laws challenged on this basis to date. With regard to higher education, the Court has held unconstitutional a New York law under which resident aliens were eligible only if they applied for citizenship or filed a statement of intent to apply as soon as they were eligible.[28] There is little question that at present discrimination against resident aliens by state institutions of higher education, whether in the award of financial assistance or in admissions, would be unconstitutional.

Some state universities discriminate against out-of-state residents by limiting their admissions to a fixed percentage of the entering class. The existing and potential constitutional limitations upon state power in this respect are probably not materially different from those on tuition differentials for residents and nonresidents discussed previously.

Handicapped and Age Discrimination

Federal statutes also prohibit institutions receiving federal financial assistance from discriminating on the basis of age.[29] Recent lower court decisions involving the handicapped provisions suggest that educational institutions wishing to continue receiving federal assistance may not discriminate in admissions on the basis of physical or mental handicaps.[30] The courts have held that such institutions have an affirmative obligation to provide handicapped persons with the special services they require to successfully complete their educational programs. It would seem to follow that an educational institution could not reject an otherwise qualified handicapped person simply on the basis that he or she will be at a disadvantage within the educational program because no special handicapped services are available. The courts have not yet indicated whether some extremely high cost special services might be exempt from this rule, but in any event it seems fairly clear at this point that, for example, persons with hearing deficiencies who would otherwise be accepted cannot be turned down on the basis of the deficiency. Instead, the school must accept the student and provide the special service. Quite obviously, if the handicap were such that it could not be counteracted by any special service, the person would not be "otherwise qualified" for admission and on that basis could be rejected. Moreover, it is important to note that the existing case law does not suggest that educational institutions are obliged to grant admission preferences to the handicapped. To repeat, all that is required is that those who would have been otherwise accepted not be rejected.

There is virtually no litigation under the recently enacted prohibition on age discrimination. Regulations have not yet been promulgated pursuant to this statute, but are expected within the next few months.

Other Admissions Criteria

Federal and state constitutional, statutory and administrative laws impose other constraints on the use by public and, to a much more limited extent, private institutions, of particular admissions criteria, but extended discussion would be inappropriate. Possibly, a public institution's admissions policy favoring unmarried individuals would be held impermissibly to burden the newly announced (or revived) federal constitutional right to marry. Any use by a public institution of political or religious criteria of admission would stand in grave constitutional danger under the First Amendment.

C. Admissions Processes

Governing boards are also subject to legal constraints in the processes through which they make and administer admissions policy and individual admissions decisions. As usual, state legislative power is greatest as to legislative institutions, though particularized statutory regulation of admissions procedures is rare.

Procedural Due Process

The most important question here is whether and to what extent the Due Process Clause of the Fourteenth Amendment requires public institutions to afford notice and/or a hearing to rejected applicants for admission. If rejected applicants have such a federal constitutional right, all public institutions and any private institution meeting the "state action" test might be obliged at least to provide a statement of reasons for rejection and perhaps to grant hearings on demand. The courts have generally not differentiated between "state action" for equal protection and due process purposes, though they may eventually. If the courts hold that due process requires rejection hearings, they would also describe the required procedure.

This branch of procedural due process law has undergone very rapid change during the past ten years. Currently, public universities may not expel or suspend a student for disciplinary infractions without providing a statement of reasons and, at least under many circumstances, affording a hearing.[31] Whether and what form of these requirements may apply to higher education applicant rejections depends upon two issues: First, does an applicant have a Fourteenth Amendment "liberty" or "property" interest in university admissions? Second, do the demands of due process differ depending upon whether the reason for deprivation is disciplinary or academic?

The answer to the first question is quite probably no for most applicants, but future developments are not easy to anticipate. A liberty interest cannot be established unless the underlying right is itself protected by the Constitution, and the Court has held that education is not such a right, or unless denial of the right would very substantially damage the applicant's future options, as if it communicated a

serious character accusation, or substantially foreclosed
the applicant's access to all higher education or a profession. Possibly an applicant rejected in unique circumstances could make the latter sort of showing, but most
rejected applicants cannot. Property interests are more
amorphous, but Supreme Court opinions currently require
a showing by the applicant of an expectation fairly based
on state law of institutional representations, and such an
expectation is very difficult to show as to institutional decisions which are basically discretionary rather than rules-
bound. Admissions policies of selective institutions would
give rise to this kind of expectation only where they include announced set criteria which guarantee admission.
Even as to such institutions, however, the applicant must
surpass a final hurdle in order to succeed in a due process
challenge. Though never having focused squarely on the
issue, the Supreme Court has clearly implied that an individual has a property interest only in government benefits
that he has "already acquired." Several lower courts, in the
same vein, have held that the property-protection requirements of due process apply only to the termination of
benefits and not to initial application, finding a greater re-
liance interest in terminees than rejected applicants, and
more persuasive administrative cost justifications for denying hearings to the latter than the former. If the courts
maintain this distinction, decisions rejecting applicants to
higher education will remain largely exempt from due
process regulation.

Even if the courts began to modify these doctrines, the
question would remain whether they would distinguish between applicants rejected for academic reasons, probably
the vast majority of rejections, and those rejected for other
reasons. Presently, hearings are required for disciplinary
expulsions and suspensions, but the lower courts have distinguished academic expulsions. Academic expulsions from
state institutions may not lawfully be "arbitrary or capri-
cious," and this probably implies that the institution must

provide a statement of reasons and have some evidence to support its action, but hearings have not so far been required. The distinction between disciplinary and academic expulsions was recently challenged in the U.S. Supreme Court.[32] The plaintiff had been dismissed from the University of Missouri medical school on the basis of her unsatisfactory performance in the clinical segment of her educational program. The Supreme Court assumed without deciding that the dismissal deprived her of a liberty or property interest, but nonetheless held that the procedures in conjunction with her dismissal satisfied the demands of due process. The procedures included advising the plaintiff that her clinical work was unsatisfactory and placing her on probationary status on this basis, and later allowing her to "appeal" to a group of seven practicing physicians, the majority of whom concurred that her clinical work was not satisfactory. Although these procedures would not have satisfied due process in the context of a disciplinary expulsion, the Court approved these "far less stringent procedural requirements in the case of an academic dismissal." The Court explained that stricter procedures were required in the disciplinary context in order to give the student a chance to avert erroneous factual assumptions and findings concerning the events at issue; whereas, an academic expulsion is based on a judgment that is "more subjective and evaluative than the typical factual questions presented in the average disciplinary decision."

The upshot of this analysis is that for now and the near future, the admissions process will probably be largely free from significant due process regulation. Even if, as seems quite unlikely, the courts were to conclude that applicants have a general "liberty" or "property" interest in admission, the informal procedures typically employed in making admissions decisions are likely to be held satisfactory for due process purposes. The types of judgments implicit in most admissions decisions are even less like disputes over historical facts than are academic expulsions.

An academic expulsion is at least normally predicated on historical events like examinations, papers or clinical performance which might serve as the basis for conflicting testimony by different "experts" at a hearing. Most run-of-the-mill rejections of applicants for admission, by comparison, are based on a statistical (or experiential) generalization as to the types of characteristics that usually correlate with future academic performance. Applicants are rarely rejected because of a factual mistake as to their posession or nonpossession of such characteristics (for example, a mistake as to their prior academic record or standardized test scores), and it is thus difficult to perceive any fact-accuracy function to be performed by hearings.

It is worth noting, finally, that future developments in access policy could themselves effect due process regulation. For example, if selective institutions accepted more students on the theory that those unable to survive academically can be expelled, the issue that now presents itself as "application-rejection" would have been transformed to "academic expulsion." In this event, some due process regulation would be likely, and the major questions would be whether and what kind of hearings might be required, although recent Supreme Court decisions suggest that minimal procedural checks would suffice.

State Administrative Procedure Requirements

Many states now have administrative procedure acts which govern the processes of all state agencies. If state institutions of higher education are held by the courts to be administrative agencies subject to administrative procedure acts, they will be bound to comply with all procedural requirements, in making both policy and particular decisions. In some states, higher education is expressly excluded from coverage by such acts. Attempted inclusion of constitutional universities could raise substantial state constitutional questions, and in general the courts are likely to interpret ambiguous acts as not intended to include them.

The position of legislative universities in the face of statutory ambiguity is less clear, and depends upon judicial interpretations which may well vary from state to state.

State Contract Law

Private institutions are not subject to the due process clause or to state administrative procedure acts. They may employ any processes permitted by their charters, and typically their discretion is great. Their relationship with students has historically been analyzed by the courts in contractual terms, and since no contract exists prior to a student's admission, they have been free to employ whatever procedures they wish in making individual admissions decisions. This contractual approach has been criticized increasingly in the legal literature, and general trends in the law of private associations may eventually lead to some kind of "reasonableness" requirement.

Restrictions on the Acquisition and Use of Information

A variety of federal and state constitutional, statutory, administrative and common law doctrines impose constraints upon the power of higher education institutions to acquire and use information from applicants bearing upon the admissions decision. The general principles of legislative and institutional authority and state action do not differ from those in other areas.

A detailed discussion here seems inappropriate. In general, institutions may require applicants to furnish any information relevant to permissible admissions criteria, and may reject a noncomplying applicant on this ground alone. Institutions probably may also request information relevant for statistical or similar use in future admissions policy formulation, though it is not clear that state institutions could reject a noncomplying applicant for this reason alone.

Statutes in several states prohibit higher education institutions from requesting information on race, creed, color, religion, and national origin. The Constitution also limits the power of public institutions to request information concerning applicants' religious or political beliefs and, up to a point, his or her organizational affiliations. The constitutional privilege against self-incrimination may impose some limits on the authority of a state institution automatically to reject an applicant who refuses to answer a question on this ground.

Privacy rights are also protected by constitutional, statutory, administrative, and common law, though the contour and character of these rights is often unclear and there can be important variations from state to state. Some privacy rights protect simply against unwanted intrusion; others against unwanted publicity. Requests for intimate information concerning family or sexual relationships, or requests of third parties like psychiatrists and physicians, when not authorized by the applicant, could face significant legal challenge even if the information were not publicized.

The most important recent development in this area has been the section of the Education Amendments of 1974, as amended,[33] which imposes federal records requirements on institutions receiving federal aid. The statute grants students the right to examine their own files, to a hearing to challenge file contents, and to the correction of inaccuracies. Only students who have attended the institution are granted these rights; rejected applicants are not. The statute also exempts certain documents from student examination: financial records of parents; most confidential letters and recommendations filed before January 1, 1975; confidential recommendations filed thereafter, if the student has signed a waiver of his right of access; records maintained by a physician, psychiatrist, or the like, and used only in connection with treatment; records of institutional personnel in the sole possession of the maker and not available to others. The waiver as to confidential recommendations cannot be made a condition for admission or financial aid. The statute also prohibits the release by the institution to others of any information in the file, unless the student gives his written and specific consent. This prohibition exempts "directory information," like height, weight and so forth, but students must be given a chance to object.

This statute, whether or not wise, is symbolic of the constant drift of educational policy making toward greater and greater centralization. It seems a very questionable use of Congress' power to regulate through the spending power, since the subject matter has at best a tenuous relation to fiscal or quality control over granted funds, on the one hand, or to some independent constitutional power of Congress, on the other. Constitutional lines in this area are almost impossible to draw, however, and the Supreme Court is likely to have small taste for the task.

1. For an excellent recent discussion of the constitutional status of the University of California, see Horowitz, "The Autonomy of the University of California Under the State Constitution," 25 *UCLA Law Rev.* 23 (1977).
2. *Dartmouth College* v.*Woodward,* 4 Wheat. 518 (1819).
3. *Pierce* v. *Society of Sisters,* 268 U.S. 510 (1925).
4. E.g., *Farrington* v. *Tokushige,* 273 U.S. 284 (1926).
5. *San Antonio Ind. School Dist.* v. *Rodriguez,* 411 U.S. 1 (1973).
6. For an interesting discussion of some innovative constitutional theories on this issue, see Strickman, "The Tuition-Poor, The Public University and Equal Protection," 29 *U. Fla. Rev.* 595 (1977).
7. 412 U.S. 441 (1973).
8. *Elkins* v.*Moreno,* 46 L.W. 4337 (1978).
9. The Supreme Court recognized but did not rule on this possibility in *Elkins* v. *Moreno,* note 8 *supra.*

10. 38 U.S.C. § 1601 *et seq.*
11. 42 U.S.C. § 402(d) and 1397(a).
12. 28 U.S.C. § 1001 *et seq.*
13. *Tilton* v. *Richardson,* 403 U.S. 672 (1971); *Hunt* v. *McNair,* 413 U.S. 734 (1973).
14. *Roemer* v. *Board of Public Works of Maryland,* 426 U.S. 736 (1976).
15. *Americans United For Separation of Church & State* v. *Blanton,* 433 F. Supp. 97 (USDC M Tenn., 1977), aff'd, 46 L.W. 3187 (1977); and *Smith* v. *Board of Governors of the University of North Carolina,* 429 F. Supp. 871 (USDC WNC, 1977) aff'd, 46 L.W. 3187 (1977).
16. I have been very much assisted in these sections by Hornby, Higher Education Admission Law Service (ETS). This Service is the best available source for legal research involving the admissions process.
17. See notes 5 and 6 *supra.*
18. See note 25 *infra.*
19. The most important recent Supreme Court decision in this area is *Jackson* v. *Metropolitan Edison Co.,* 419 U.S. 345 (1974).
20. 42 U.S.C. § 2000e.
21. *Washington* v. *Davis,* 426 U.S. 229 (1976).
22. 416 U.S. 312 (1974).
23. 18 Cal. 3d 34, 553 P.2d 1152 (1976); cert. granted, 429 U.S. 1090 (1977).
23a. See Rev. Rul. 71-447, *1971 Int. Rev. Bull. No. 40,* at 10.
24. 42 U.S.C. § 2000d (1970).
24a. It should be emphasized, however, that under the so-called "pin-point" provisions of the federal statute, the offending "school, college, or department" must itself be the recipient of federal funds. See 42 U.S.C. § 2000d-1, 20 U.S.C. § 1682, and § 1681(c). Thus, for example, if racially preferential programs are held to be discriminatory under the statute, a law school program would not come within the prohibition of the statute simply because other parts of the university were receiving federal assistance. The law school itself would have to be a recipient of federal assistance. Moreover, at least one lower court has held that the amount of federal assistance must be significant before the statute will be held applicable in private lawsuits, although other lower courts have decided this issue differently. Compare *Stewart* v. *New York University,* 430 F. Supp. 1305 (S.D.N.Y. 1976), with

Flanagan v. *President & Directors of Georgetown College,* 417 F. Supp. 377 (D.C.D.C. 1976).

25. 429 U.S. 190 (1976).
26. Last term the Supreme Court did review one lower court decision involving single-sex educational institutions, but affirmed the lower court decision by an equally divided Court. *Vorchheimer* v. *School District of Philadelphia,* 430 U.S. 703 (1977). This means that among the eight Justices participating, four of them believed single-sex institutions were legal and four believed they were illegal. Mr. Justice Rehnquist did not participate in the consideration of the case, but examination of his opinions on related issues would lead one to guess that he would vote to uphold single-sex institutions, and on this basis to predict that a majority of the current Court will eventually take this position.
27. 20 U.S.C. § 1681(a) (1974).
28. *Nyquist* v. *Mauclet,* 432 U.S. ____ (1977).
29. 29 U.S.C. § 794.
30. See, *Barnes* v. *Converse College,* 436 F. Supp. 635 (1977); *Davis* v. *Southeastern Community College, CCH Poverty Law Reporter* ¶ 25,836.
31. See e.g., *Dixon* v. *Alabama Board of Education,* 294 F. 2d 150 (5th Cir. 1961).
32. *Bd. of Curators of University of Missouri* v. *Horowitz,* 38 *CCH S. Ct. Bull.* p. B943 (U.S. Sup. Ct., 1978).

A REVIEW OF U.S. ADMISSIONS POLICIES AND PRACTICES

Alice J. Irby
Rutgers University

A REVIEW OF U.S. ADMISSIONS POLICIES AND PRACTICES

My remarks fall into three categories: (1) a review of access to higher education in the 20th century from a U.S. perspective; (2) admissions policies within the context of institutional policies and planning; and (3) admissions practices and their impact on access.

U.S. Perspective on Access

Colleges and universities in the United States reflect the values, stresses, and demands of the society. Though they function as critics of and innovators for the society, they are at the same time very much a part of it. Thus while higher education in America entered the 20th century largely dominated by the aristocratic traditional influences of an earlier time, it soon began to reflect currents in the society toward the broadening of educational opportunity. There was a move away from the premise of the intellectually elite that only a few are able to benefit from education, toward a commitment to make education available to all citizens who might profit from it. This was evidenced in the development of land-grant colleges following the passage of the Morrill Act in 1862.[1]

When higher education focused at the turn of the century on accommodating the "able few," requirements for admission to colleges were stated in terms of achievement in specific high school subjects. Some colleges accepted virtually anyone who could afford to attend, for there was little or no financial aid to students at the time. Others required evidence of adequate performance in courses that had been specified in detail by universities. Gradually, emphasis moved away from defining the content of specific high school courses to measure the qualitative performance in broader academic areas and to subject matter examinations. Colleges not using common examinations opened their doors to all who could afford to enroll or depended upon high school credits and grades as reported by secondary schools to admit students. Public institutions, e.g., state universities and land-grant colleges, relied primarily upon high school credits and grades.

Underlying these academic requirements was the assumption that below some minimum standard of ability and achievement students could not benefit from college and consequently should not be admitted. Rather than adjusting institutional policies, and consequently, the size of the student body, to enroll all those who might succeed, some colleges used minimum admissions requirements as a rationale for limiting the freshman class to a predetermined size. Few institutions rejected large numbers of applicants, however, and gestures toward selectivity in the first part of the century gave way in the 1930s to vigorous recruiting to attract enough students to keep college doors open.

The end of World War II signaled the beginning of what is known as selective admissions, in both the public and private sectors. Institutions could not expand rapidly enough to accept all those who would have qualified in the past. A number of colleges did not plan expansion as part of their goals. During the 1950s and well into the 1960s, the demand for entry into a number of colleges exceeded the capacity of the institutions to accommodate all qualified students.

In the 1960s, the forces of expansion accelerated. There was an increasing availability of funds for college buildings, libraries, developmental research projects, faculty recruitment and reward, and student grants and loans. This growth came about as a matter of public policy and most of the growth occurred in the public institutions. In 1955 the opening enrollment of degree credit students in all institutions was 2,678,623. In 1964-65, it was 4,550,173 and in 1974-75, 8,491,000. The nondegree credit student population has increased even faster, from 329,847 in 1964-65 to 1,770,000 in 1974-75.

The factors resulting in greater access to higher education have been part of an expanding national search for talent. Awakened in the mid-1950s to the waste of human resources in relation to the national need for broadly educated and highly skilled people, America's first response was to increase the spaces available in the college classrooms and dormitories so that the millions of students could be accommodated.

Four dominant underlying factors contributing to the expansion were: the wealth of the economy, the democratization of the society, the manpower needs of a technological society, and the orbiting of Sputnik in the late 1950s. The commitment to expanding free or inexpensive educational opportunity beyond secondary school to all who could benefit was exemplified in the growth of the four-year state colleges and the public comprehensive junior colleges.

To facilitate growth, Congress provided increased funds via scholarships and loans. For example, the College Work Study Program, established in 1964, and the Guaranteed Student Loan program and Equal Opportunity Grant program incorporated in the Higher Education Act of 1965 were added to the already significant loan program initiated in 1958 under the National Educational Defense Act. In 1955-56 the total amount of financial assistance available to students in postsecondary institutions was estimated to be around $96 million. By 1974-75, this amount had grown to nearly $6.5 billion.

Another sign of change was the blurring of the sharp breaking point between secondary school and college.

Education was described as a cradle-to-grave affair. The somewhat arbitrary point of transition, i.e., from high school to college, was modified by such practices as admitting to college older students and students without high school diplomas, enrolling well-prepared students in upper-level college courses on the basis of demonstrated proficiency, the expansion of evening and weekend programs for adults and part-time students, and the development of "universities without walls."

As a result of these changes and trends, higher education in the United States can be characterized by the following:

a. **The diversity of institutions:**

There are public and private colleges; large and small colleges; universities; two- and four-year colleges, technical institutes. The ages of the institutions range from those founded in the mid-1700s, such as Rutgers and Princeton, and the oldest state university established in 1789, to several hundred institutions that are less than 20 years old.

b. **The lack of a uniform federal system of education at the secondary and higher educational levels:**

There's great variability among states. Since this is the case and there has been no federal system of secondary education in the United States, most education has been "a state affair." Some states have highly centralized education systems; others have autonomous school districts and institutions of higher education. Public support is greater in some states than in others.

c. **The pluralism of the larger society:**

Higher education is part of that pluralism. Though some would argue that equality has not been institutionalized in this society, the channels of opportunity have certainly not been fixed. Pathways to success have been increasingly variable. Therefore, a system of higher education that may appear to be somewhat haphazard does attempt to maximize freedom of choice and the availability of alternatives. Perhaps such freedom and availability necessitates some inefficiency.

d. The same tensions that are reflected in the entire society: Some of the major tensions that are experienced are between equality and competition. The notions of equal opportunity, equality before the law, equal status—these may in the extreme lead to ignoring differences among individuals and to denying any inequalities in capacity and ability, which may in turn lead to mediocrity. On the other hand, competition or the notion of "let the best man win," and the evaluation and appreciation of individual performance may in the extreme result in the rule of the jungle—raw striving, aggressiveness, and brutality.

In any event, the 20th century has seen in higher education in the United States a movement away from the restrictive to the expansive; away from availability to those who could conform to the structure to changing the structure; and away from the idea of an intellectual elite to education available to all who could profit from it.

States have dealt with these issues in different ways and over different periods of time. The expansion of higher education has led to increased emphasis on statewide planning and coordination. Some people thought coordination began with the first coordinating board established some years ago. Such was not the case; coordination of some kind took place in every state either through the governor's office or the legislature.

Agencies such as coordinating or statewide governing boards have developed, in part, because of the need to engage in long-term planning to (a) optimize the distribution of education to the citizens of the state, and (b) to maximize the use of resources. Among the states there have also been differences in the treatment of public and private institutions. For example, private higher education has always been an important and dominant factor in Massachusetts. In the south, midwest, and much of the west, such is not the case.

The development of multiple state systems of higher education had differential impacts on admissions and

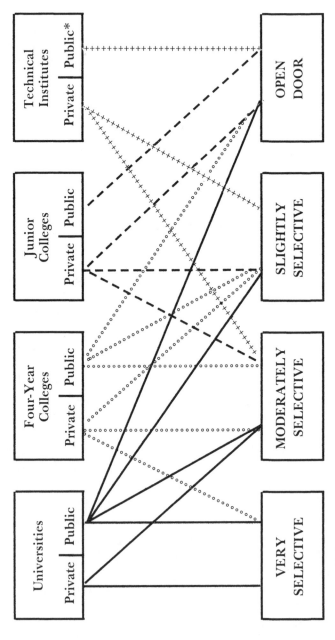

*Some programs in public community colleges have become selective because the demand for places exceeds the resources available. Such programs are usually technical or professional, e.g. nursing.

access to higher education. Compare, for example, the California system with an admissions policy for the top 12 percent going to university, the top third to the state colleges, and the open door community colleges with that of New Jersey in which there has been much more fluidity in the admissions policies among state institutions. There will be more discussion of this later.

The result of this growth and selectivity has been the development of several types of institutions and admissions policies that are found within these institutions. This can be shown in an oversimplified fashion in the chart on page 12.

Though confusing to the eye, the graph is intended to depict the variability in admissions policies among the various kinds of institutions. The institutions in a given category cannot be described simply by a single admissions policy.

It is important to make two points:

It should be noted that selectivity in admissions is not synonymous with institutional quality. While it is true that highly selective colleges and universities are usually centers of excellence, it does not follow that less selective institutions are of inferior quality. The existence of some excellent open door state colleges and universities is testimony to this fact.

The matter of choosing a college is initially the student's. Whatever the admissions policy of a particular institution, the student selects the college to a greater extent than the college selects the student. The college can veto but the student initiates; in that sense he selects the college. Recruiting programs at colleges (even the selective ones), the marshalling of alumni to search for students, and the concern exhibited over the public images projected by colleges attest to this fact.

Institutional Policies and Planning

Admissions policies are set within the context of institutional and statewide planning. My comments pertain primarily to the public sector, specifically states in which there is coordination and planning between a state coordinating agency and the institutions.

A. Many institutions develop master plans for their growth and development. Usually these are ten-year plans. State coordinating agencies set goals and objectives for the development of higher education and frequently take the initiative in establishing statewide, long-term enrollment estimates.

In New Jersey, setting enrollment targets (a major influence on admissions policies) is critical to short-term institutional planning, because in New Jersey the budgets for state institutions are tied to enrollment goals. Let me explain how this works. (See attached chart.)

The first enrollment estimates for the fall of 1975 were made 18 months prior to that time, in December 1973. Those estimates, which were recommendations from the deans of units of the universities, were revised by the university administration in February 1974 and submitted as part of the budget document in the summer of 1974. Once students enrolled in the fall of 1974, estimates for the fall of 1975 were revised on the basis of actual enrollments in September.

Occasionally these estimates are revised a second time in January or February. This makes precise forecasting of enrollments difficult and the forecasts include, invariably, errors of estimation which may be random rather than systematic in a given direction.[2]

There are two general categories of students that must be taken into account: those who are enrolled in the spring semester and continue into the next fall and those students who are not in the university at all during the given academic year but come to the university either as new students or returning students in the following academic year. The second category is difficult to predict since it includes several subcategories: (a) new students who never attended the university before; (b) students who drop out and return after one or two semesters; (c) transfers within the university from one unit of the university to another.

Now what goes into these estimates?

1. The opinions of the deans of the schools and colleges. This is especially important with respect to the professional schools at the undergraduate and graduate levels.

2. Estimates of demand for access by students. General knowledge about the population pool from which students come, e.g. the graduating population of New Jersey high schools, the proportion of high school graduates going on to college, the graduating population of community colleges.

3. Present and past admissions policies and changes in those policies in view of changes in the demand for higher education and changes in institutional or state policy.

   For example, if there is a change in university policy to encourage part-time students to come into graduate programs, enrollment estimates will reflect that change in policy.

   Another example. If it appears that a unit is admitting students who are having great difficulty in meeting the requirements of the faculty of that unit, they will establish an enrollment goal that will require different standards for admission than the next year and vice versa.

4. Long-term population trends, i.e., the number and proportion of high school graduates going on to college.

5. Manpower requirements for professions such as engineering, nursing, and law.

6. Staff and faculty resources required to meet the enrollment estimates. Example: If there are problems in the present distribution of resources, and these can-

not be changed in one year, our enrollment goals will be altered to prevent unnecessary dislocation of staff.

7. Empirical data describing past experience, e.g., attrition, male/female composition, full-time/part-time composition, space available, plans for capital development.

Once these headcount targets are set, the new student goals are broken down to freshmen, transfer students, and students to be readmitted.

Ten-year projections are made at the same time and these are revised annually.

Each semester, after the students have registered, the actual enrollments are compared to the estimated and budgeted enrollment. Funds for operating budgets in public four-year institutions in New Jersey are tied to the budgeted enrollment and are adjusted subsequently to reflect the actual enrollments in relation to the budgeted number.

B. One can see the impact on admission's policy of setting enrollment targets in this way. For example, if institutions have excess space they are likely to adopt policies of open admissions or to relax previous admissions standards, assuming the operating resources are available to provide instruction for the students. If, on the other hand, the unit must reduce the number of students, this usually means reducing the number of freshmen or transfer students. Consequently they are likely to become more restrictive in their admissions policies. From the standpoint of the state it is important not to overbuild, that is, to increase the numbers of spaces available beyond the population that will be entering higher education. Or, planning may require that excess capacity be developed in the short run in order to provide for long-term growth. To date, we in the United States have had little experience in dealing with retrenchment either in terms of budget or numbers of students. Planning for large swings in population growth as it relates to higher education is relatively new to us.

Finally, revisions in enrollment goals as related to available spaces may lead to competition among institutions for students. On the other hand, if the enrollment goals lead to restrictive policies there may be charges of exclusion and elitism since the demand for education in a particular unit cannot be met.

Admissions Policies and Practices

This section deals first with institutional policies and then with the process and practices of admissions offices in institutions of higher education.

A. Policies are set in a variety of ways:

1. Community colleges usually follow a policy of open door admissions and enrollment targets flow from the admissions policy that is set.

2. At the other extreme, well-known private universities such as Princeton adopt an institutional policy which restricts admission to the best prepared students in the United States and results in a highly selective admission policy. Princeton has made the decision to remain small, relative to many public institutions, and national in its search for able students; most state institutions choose to concentrate on serving the needs of the population of that state.

3. A state such as California sets a specific admissions policy and then attempts to build its community colleges, state colleges, and universities to distribute the population according to that policy. For example, the top 12 percent of the high school class can be admitted to the universities, the top third of the high school classes can go to the state colleges, and the community colleges are open to all students.

4. In Rutgers, and I imagine in some of the state colleges, admissions policies are set through a combination of collegiate interests, university administration policies, and state policies with respect to budget approval. The university administration exerts pressure on admissions policies by setting the enrollment

targets, in consultation with the deans, for each college. The university gives leeway to the colleges, with review and advice by university officers, to set admissions standards within the total enrollment goal. The university initiates policy discussions among the deans and the university admissions policy committee. The situation in a university like Rutgers with its various units is much more fluid and the policies are more diverse than in other universities with more homogeneous collegiate units.

B.   A few words now about the process:

First let me discuss the flow of information about students from one institution to another. I will concentrate on the process from high school into college or university, although essentially the same procedures are used for students transferring from one college to another and from college into graduate and professional school. Somewhat different procedures are used for adults and part-time students. Secondary schools have information on candidates, descriptions of courses, and objective data about performance in school, i.e., high school grades and rank in graduating class. This information is forwarded to the colleges by (a) the students, and (b) school officials. The colleges require an application by the student, information from the school, particularly the school transcript, and recommendations from the principal or the guidance counselor. Many public and private four-year institutions require scores on an entrance examination such as the SAT* or ACT*. The test information comes to the college directly from the testing agency.

All of this begins to come together in the fall of the senior year in high school. Sometimes students apply at the end of their junior year and are admitted as early decision candidates. In such cases, the junior-year test scores and three-year high school records are used for admissions purposes. Frequently in open door institutions, applications are received all year and many of

*Scholastic Aptitude Test or American College Testing Program.

them come to the colleges in late spring, summer, on up to registration in the fall. Moreover, in some of the community colleges, tests are not required before entry but are used as placement vehicles at the time of entry.

The admissions office itself is usually made up of a director or dean of admissions and staff that engage in interviewing students, visiting students in schools and alumni at home, and reviewing applications. There is usually at least one admissions committee made up of faculty and administrators. In large universities, there may be an admissions committee for each school. These committees may function in one of several ways: to develop policies and to review the implementation of those policies; as a resource and advisory group to the director or dean of admissions; as a committee to review marginal or difficult applications; or as a committee to review all cases.

Recruitment means different things in different institutions. Sometimes in colleges in need of students, particularly small private colleges, the recruiter is used to persuade students of the benefit of coming to his institution. State colleges and universities use recruiters as people to keep the secondary schools informed and to discourage students who will be unlikely to complete programs in these institutions. The prestigious institutions, such as Princeton and Harvard, use recruitment to get the best candidates, to give accurate information about the institution, and to guarantee a national pool of candidates. The timing of these visits either to other college campuses, secondary schools, or alumni organizations takes place in the spring of the junior year or the fall of the senior year.

C. The decision-making process:

Some of the factors that contribute to admissions policies and to admissions decisions include the following:

sex
place of residence

religious affiliation
ability to pay
evidence of leadership, community activities,
    special interests and abilities
past academic performance
future promise based on aptitude test scores.

In most state institutions the critical variables are place of residence, past academic performance, and test scores. Admissions officers use what I call either an actuarial or a clinical approach to the decision-making process. Sometimes admissions officers try to balance the two approaches. An actuarial approach would involve combining the objective indices such as test scores, high school grades, rank in class, in some fashion which puts the students in rank order in terms of ability, preparation, and potential. For example, an institution may use a cutoff on test scores and/or high school records separately, or they may combine statistically these indices to yield a prediction of future performance. The clinical approach involves the subjective examination of the information in a student's record. Statistical information is reviewed along with information about the activities of the student, the recommendations that might be in the student's file, the personal characteristics that are revealed through interviews. As already said, in many admissions offices it is necessary to reject some proportion of applicants. This forces the admissions staff or admissions committee to establish criteria for discriminating among those candidates seeking entrance.

In some institutions, a premium is placed on impartiality, and objective measures such as high school grades, test scores and specific academic requirements have been used to rank order applicants and to apply cutoff points in line with available spaces. Such a policy is impartial but it also implies validity which does not exist in such objective measures. Much more, these measures do not account for many of the global and specialized qualities that contribute to successful experiences in college. In other colleges, admissions committees search for clues about the character, interests and aspirations of students that might be combined with objective data in order to make decisions. While there is genuine concern about assessing fairly the impact of differences in socioeconomic levels and motivation, little is known about how to treat such differences. Thus, admissions decisions, though thoughtful and sincere, are sometimes based partially on ignorance, hunches, and falacious opinions.

Implicit in making judgments and choices is the idea that the judges can identify those who are potentially successful or best among the able. In fact, the art is not precise, which serves to underscore the ambiguities and harsh realities of college admissions. Sprinkled with reason and a degree of order the admissions process is nevertheless characterized by uncertainty and limited by imperfect knowledge. The ambiguities are somewhat more understandable when one realizes that in addition to selecting students using imperfect tools and knowledge, the admissions officer must juggle and balance the sometimes divergent needs of the institution and of the applicants it seeks to serve.

Sorting and guiding individuals in society to maximize their potential and to fulfill society's needs is a very serious business. That is much of the business of the educational world. Educational institutions and the people in them cannot avoid making qualitative judgments about human beings whether in teaching, counseling, or promoting faculty and staff. Such measurements as rank in class, high school averages and test scores can help, but they cannot do the entire job. Blind and excessive dependence on effective but limited tools or rigidity in admissions policies and procedures may leave much of what we are about in the same condition as "Lucky Chiquita," the heroine of a Latin proverb,

"Lucky Chiquita, she was shot 12 times;
But only 5 proved fatal."

SAMPLE ENROLLMENT ESTIMATES
RUTGERS UNIVERSITY, NEW JERSEY

	Headcount Enrollment Fall 1974 Actual	Headcount Enrollment Fall 1974 Estimated	Returning Students Fall 1974 Estimated
Camden A & S	2,833	3,000	1,735
Cook	2,097	2,235	1,467
Douglass	3,587	3,613	2,509
Engineering	998	1,200	656
Livingston	3,342	3,400	1,883
NCAS	3,867	4,175	2,400
Nursing	448	450	326
Pharmacy	669	670	470
Rutgers College	6,520	6,900	4,609
University College	8,016	8,200	4,914
Total Undergraduate	32,377	33,843	20,969
Graduate School	5,395	5,838	4,046
Business	1,339	1,420	679
Criminal Justice	53	90	26
Education	2,503	2,500	1,770
Library Service	409	375	211
Psychology	41	100	37
Social Work	850	825	497
Law—Camden	518	550	325
—Evening Law Camden	—	75	0
Law—Newark	703	750	465
—Evening Law Newark	—	75	0
	11,811	12,595	8,056
Other	281	250	131
GRAND TOTAL	44,469	46,691	29,156

NOT OFFICIAL: Used for illustrative purposes only. Prepared by the Vice President for Student Services April 30, 1975

NEW STUDENTS AND READMITTED STUDENTS
-------------------------------- Fall 1975 -----------------------------

Totals	Freshmen	Transfers	Readmits
1,265	600	450	215
768	460	150	158
1,104	841	110	53
544	430	50	64
1,517	850	550	117
1,775	960	500	315
124	78	95	49
200	145	0	55
2,291	1,800	250	241
3,286	-------------- Does not apply -----------------		
1,792			
741			
64			
730			
164			
63		Does not apply	
328			
225			
75			
285			
75			
4,542			
119			
17,535			

The issue of access in a system of higher education as compared with a single institution of higher education is the issue of balancing the need and demand for various kinds of education among a population with the resources that a state can commit as a result of its wealth, public policy, and commitment on the part of the people. To insure this balance, some schools will inevitably be selective in their admissions policies, others open door in their admissions policies. Some will move from one policy to another. The important thing is that institutional policies and practices change in order to be responsive to society's needs and to maximize human potential.

COLLEGE ADMISSIONS TESTING IN THE UNITED STATES

Jenne K. Britell
William B. Schrader
Educational Testing Service

COLLEGE ADMISSIONS
TESTING IN THE
UNITED STATES

Prior to the 20th century, U.S. institutions of higher education had extremely varied admissions policies. Some required only a high school diploma. Others, with more applicants than places, gave preference to state residents. Still others, including many of the older eastern colleges, required all applicants to take a series of tests for admissions which each college constructed. If an applicant applied to several colleges in this group, he took admissions tests for each. Only in this fashion, it was felt, would a college know whether the individual was adequately prepared to study at that institution. Different colleges required different content preparation at the secondary level. In Latin, for example, one college might require an applicant to have read Ovid; another might require Horace. There was no common syllabus on which students were examined.

In 1899, a number of these colleges met and decided that it would be more efficient for institutions and more equitable for students if a single comprehensive essay examination, which tested knowledge based on a common curriculum, were given in each subject. This examination, which would be accepted by all of the member institutions, would be developed and graded by a single group of examiners.

In 1900, these colleges formed the College Entrance Examination Board, and two of the Board's early objectives were agreement on a common syllabus and the subsequent development, administration, and grading of the single examination in each subject. The College Board's examinations, which measured students' levels of knowledge acquired through formal study of the subject and developed by college and high school teachers in the discipline, were termed *achievement* examinations.

At the time that these new examinations came into prominence—during the first 20 years of the 20th century—American psychologists, many schooled in Germany and England, were conducting research which seemed to indicate that certain learned skills or aptitudes were related to performance in various academic areas. In 1926, the College Board, by now an expanded number of institutions, developed and administered the Scholastic Aptitude Test (SAT). In contrast to the achievement examinations which measured knowledge gained through study of a particular subject, the SAT was designed to measure verbal and quantitative aptitude—skills learned and developed over an extended period of time through both school and other experiences and less closely tied to a particular curriculum.

Although the achievement examinations were given in essay form, the SAT was presented in the objective form and could be scored readily by clerks and later by machines. As the 20th century progressed, U.S. colleges and later graduate schools, faced with an expanding pool of applicants representing the heterogeneous U.S. population, relied increasingly on these tests. Continuing research showed that scores on the tests related to the ability to do [first year] college or graduate work, and they provided a single measure for evaluating applicants from diverse educational backgrounds with which an admissions officer might not be familiar. These admissions tests were instrumental in changing the population in the highly selective colleges from one homogeneous in socioeconomic background and heterogeneous in ability to one homogeneous in ability but heterogeneous in socioeconomic background.

In the 1940s, the College Board moved to an objective form of the achievement tests and this, too, could be scored by clerks and subsequently by machine. In 1948 the College Board, the American Council on Education, and the Carnegie Foundation for the Advancement of Teaching, all of which had sponsored different testing programs, founded the Educational Testing Service (ETS) to assume their testing activities and to carry on research requisite to the further development of measurement programs. The College Board, which sets policy for the SAT and Achievement tests, now numbers over 2,000 public and private secondary schools, school systems, two- and four-year colleges and universities, and educational associations. Under the sponsorship of groups representing the educational constituencies which use the test, ETS also develops and administers three major testing programs used in the admissions process in U.S. graduate education. These are: the Graduate Management Admission Test, for the Admission Council for Graduate Study in Management, an association of 41 graduate schools of business; the Graduate Record Examinations, for the Graduate Record Examinations Board, an association of U.S. graduate schools in the arts and sciences; and the Law School Admission Test, for the Law School Admission Council, an association of some 160 American law schools.

The Nature of Tests

Today, despite the presence of more varied educational programs, objective verbal and quantitative aptitude tests and achievement tests remain central to the college and graduate school admissions process in the United States. This is so because the verbal and quantitative measures seem to predict academic success in a very wide variety of fields of study. Contemporary verbal aptitude tests usually measure ability to read standard American English with understanding and to use verbal relationships, e.g., to choose the word most nearly opposite in meaning to the specified word. Quantitative (mathematical) aptitude tests measure ability to handle various quantitative relationships, to understand graphs, and to read materials dealing with quantitative relationships.

Although these abilities are relevant to performance in a number of academic areas, it is important to remember that, like skills in a particular discipline, they are *learned* skills, and both are developed through the process of education. As would be expected, most students who earn high scores on quantitative aptitude tests do well on mathematic achievement tests. The value of the aptitude-achievement distinction arises primarily from the guidance it offers in test interpretation when the scores do not in fact agree.

Although a variety of other aptitudes have been identified by psychologists, including aptitudes for dealing with spatial relations and using abstract reasoning, research to date has not shown that these skills make a useful contribution to predicting academic performance, beyond the information already provided by the verbal and quantitative scores.

A great deal of research has been devoted to efforts to measure motivation, creativity, leadership, and other characteristics which appear to relate to subsequent achievement. Some success has been achieved in research settings. However, the transition from use in research to operational use in college admissions practices has not occurred, although some admissions officers may try to assess these characteristics informally through interviews or letters of recommendation. To some extent, lack of consensus on both the nature and means of measuring these characteristics has probably hindered their acceptance. Biographical data of past performance and success play an important part in the admissions process, but efforts to systematize use and evaluation of this material by developing quantitative indexes on biographical data have as yet had little or no impact on college admissions. Finally, considerable success has been achieved in measuring interests by summarizing self-reported data on various detailed interests into a form more convenient for interpretation. The use of these interest measures, however, is largely restricted to educational and vocational guidance, since a student eager to gain admission may readily distort his answers to present what he considers to be a favorable picture of himself.

Although both the early admissions tests of individual colleges and the initial academic achievement tests of the College Board were in essay form, for the past 30 years college and graduate admissions tests in the United States have been primarily objective in form. In other areas of education, in the United States as elsewhere, the essay test remains the traditional form of measuring educational outcomes. The essay test enables the student to display the depth of knowledge he or she possesses. At the same time the essay examination places a heavy demand on the grader who must read and judge the merits of the essay. In addition, the essay examination may not produce consistent grading processes since there is often lack of agreement among readers over the merits of a single essay.

The development and use of the essay test lightens the work of the test developer but increases that of the grader. In contrast, the objective test rquires extensive research and definition in the test construction process and lessens the burden on the grader. Because the major part of the intellectual work in objective testing is done prior to the test administration, this form is particularly well suited to large-scale testing programs, such as the college and graduate school admissions examinations in the United States.

The development process of objective aptitude and achievement tests involves clear specification of the questions, classification according to type and difficulty, and distribution of the different kinds of questions, so that there are an appropriate number of each kind and level of difficulty. Different but parallel forms (in terms of content and level of difficulty) can be developed through test specification, pretest of questions to identify defects in their formulation, and subsequent statistical analysis to assure that the forms are parallel. In the objective test, the tasks presented to the student are sharply defined, and the student's performance can be scored in a strictly mechanical way by clerks or machines. In each question, the student is asked to choose only the best answer from a set of defined possible answers.

The balance between objective and essay testing in the college admissions process reflects the usefulness of both kinds of tests in measuring educational outcomes. Essay test grades contribute significantly to the admissions decisions because essays are used widely in secondary schools and therefore exert great influence on high school grades, the most critical single factor in the admissions process. Both essay and modern objective tests can measure the student's ability to analyze, to apply knowledge, and to comprehend complex issues. Although the essay test permits the student to display depth and extent of knowledge, the objective test permits the measuring of many candidates along certain dimensions equally. The essay test, although closer to real life tasks, can suffer from the difference between graders' opinions and covers only a limited area of knowledge. Because a large number of objective questions can be answered in the time allotted, the examiner can obtain a relatively comprehensive knowledge of the student's strengths and weaknesses. Finally, objective tests are more likely to be truly a *standardized* examination—systematically measuring the same qualities via the same instrument for all individuals. However, they are less likely to sample high-level skills.

With either form of test—essay or objective—three major issues merit consideration:

the *reliability* of the test—its precision as a measuring instrument;

the *validity* of the test—its relevance for the performance of specific tasks under specific circumstances, or the extent to which it measures what it is intended to measure;

the *appropriate use* of the test.

Because the tests most widely used in the college admissions process in the United States are standardized, objective tests of verbal and quantitative aptitude (either the SAT, developed and administered by ETS for the College Board or those of the American College Testing Program), the discussion which follows will focus primarily on these tests in relation to issues of precision, relevance, and appropriate use.

Precision of Measurement

When tests are scored objectively, the precision of measurement—the reliability of the test for a defined group of students—can be determined statistically. Statistical methods also exist for determining how accurately scores on a particular test predict average grades in university X—the predictive validity of the test. Further, statistical analysis can provide information on the extent to which the accuracy of the prediction can be improved by combining test scores with high school grade point average, rather than using either grade point average (GPA) or test scores alone. The results of this research have important implications for the ways in which test scores can and should be used.

In evaluating the precision of a test, it is important to remember that all forms of measurement are subject to statistical error—random, unpredictable variation. The random errors inherent in test scores must be small relative to the real differences among those who are tested if the scores are to be useful. For this reason, comparisons of the random error with the variation of those examined should be made for each intended use of the test. There are various ways of describing the degree of measurement error: they differ only in respect to the aspect of measurement error with which they are concerned.

The first, the *reliability coefficient,* expresses precision in terms of a correlation. This indicates the degree to which two measures of ability for the same group of people agree and are consistent. Suppose that two different versions (Form A and Form B) of a verbal aptitude test are developed. Each version would have the same number of questions and would be given with the same time limit. As discussed earlier, every effort would be made through the test construction process to ensure that the same general abilities were being measured and that the difficulty levels of the two tests were equal. Through the pretest of questions and subsequent analysis, defective questions would be eliminated from the two. Although the two versions would contain entirely different questions, they can be thought of as parallel forms of the same test.

If all students took both forms, how closely would the relative standing of students on Form A match the relative standing of the students on Form B? If there are only trivial differences in relative standing, both forms are obviously measuring the same thing, and each test yields a precise measure of whatever the test measures. In this instance, the reliability coefficient, the index used to measure the extent of similarity between the relative standings, would be high, indicating a close degree of relationship, or *correlation,* between the two sets of measures for the same group. A well-defined and carefully constructed aptitude test should yield a correlation coefficient of .90 or higher. There is no single reliability for all ETS examinations, since the reliability depends on the variability of the tested group. However, the SAT-Verbal and the SAT-Mathematical each has a reliability of about .90.

The closeness of relationship represented by a reliability coefficient of .90 can be illustrated by describing the standing on the second test (Form B) by students who score in the top fifth on the first test (Form A). It would be expected that about 75 percent would score in the top fifth, about 25 percent in the middle three-fifths, and virtually none in the bottom fifth. The degree of agreement between the two tests, although certainly not perfect, is generally considered to be an acceptable standard for a single test which is to be used along with other information in making admissions decisions about individuals.

The concept of parallel forms, built to the same specifications with respect to abilities measured and level of difficulty, has highly practical as well as theoretical implications. Scores on different parallel forms can be made interchangeable so that scores earned on Form A can be compared with scores earned on Form B. Accordingly, different test forms can be given at different test administrations without inconvenience to the user or unfairness to the student. It is possible, moreover, for a college or univeristy to compare the ability level of its applicants and enrolled students from year to year, even though new forms are introduced. Students who cannot attend a regular administration may be given a different form at a later date and earn scores which need not be distinguished from scores earned at the regular administration.

In practice, an additional step is taken in reporting scores in order to increase comparability of scores on different forms of the same test. This process, called equating, provides a way of adjusting scores on each new form to make them consistent with a continuing reported score scale over previous years. The result of equating is usually a simple linear equation which defines the reported score corresponding to each possible score on the form. If two tests measure the same abilities, but differ substantially in difficulty level, it may be necessary to use a curvilinear relationship to equate scores on the two tests.

Another way of determining the precision of a particular test as a measurement instrument is through the standard error of measurement. The actual score on a test can be conceived as the sum of the student's "true score" and "error." The "true score" is the theoretical average of an infinitely large number of measurements on a single individual on parallel forms of the test. The "error" is the amount by which the obtained score differs from the true score. For the SAT-Verbal, the standard error of measurement is about 32 points on a scale running from 200 (low) to 800 (high). For the SAT-Mathematical, the standard error of measurement is about 36 points on a similar scale. The standard error of measurement indicates the amount of variation in scores to be expected when the same student takes different forms of the test. In contrast to the reliability coefficient, the lower the standard error of measurement, the greater the precision of the test. Two-thirds of the time, a student will score within one standard error of measurement of his true score.

Because the reliability of essay grades depends on the readers and on the grading process, research on this topic is not readily summarized or generalized. Most of the work has centered on how closely different readers agree in evaluating the same paper; that is, on reader reliability. A satisfactory degree of agreement can be achieved by selection and training of readers and by developing a consensus on grading standards for a particular question. The reader reliability of writing tests has received a great deal of attention during the past 50 years. In one representative study,* on each of five days each selected paper ($n = 25$) was given to 25 different readers. Reader reliability for a single reader (that is, the extent to which the grades he assigned correlated with those assigned by another single reader) was .41; for two, .58; for four, .73. Even if four readers evaluated a student's paper, there was a considerable variation among different sets of readers in grading the same paper.

---

*A. E. Myers, Carolyn B. McConville, and W. E. Coffman, *Reliability of Reading of the College Board English Composition Test, December 1963.* College Entrance Examination Board Research and Development Report 64-5, No. 3, Princeton, N.J.: Educational Testing Service, 1964.

The Relation of Test Scores to School Record and University Success—Their Validity

The acceptance of aptitude tests in the United States was greatly facilitated by the fact that for a long period all candidates who took College Board Achievement Tests also took the SAT. Because universities sought to accept students from throughout the United States and were unwilling to limit admissions to applicants from schools with grading standards and programs they knew well, aptitude test scores were a valuable supplement to the school record and achievement test scores. Clearly the same verbal and quantitative abilities which produce high scores on the aptitude test would be advantageous to earning high grades in high schools, and high school studies would develop further the abilities measured by the tests. To a considerable extent, then, test scores and grades measure the same skills. However, scores do provide an additional perspective on the student. Their value is enhanced by the fact that they are not dependent on the particular school that a student attends and especially by their independence of the school's particular grading standards (hard or easy). High scoring students are found in a great variety of schools.

When a test is to be used, the abilities which it measures must be related to the task that is involved, or the test is inappropriate. The relationship of scores to school record and to university success refers to their *validity*, the correlation between one set of accomplishments—the school or university record—and the test scores. Relationship does not mean causation—only that there is a tendency for the two measures to vary together. This can be positive, varying in the same direction, or negative, varying in opposite directions. The validity coefficient, like the reliability coefficient, expresses the degree of relationship between the two qualities. The presence or absence of validity can be determined only through research.

There are different kinds of validities which pertain to the relevance of subject areas, to general hypotheses, and to tasks occurring at different points in time.

Content validity refers to the matching between a particular set of educational results and the tasks presented to the student by the test. One effective method of ensuring content validity calls for giving the responsibility for defining the scope and content of the test in a particular subject to a committee of highly qualified teachers. The committee carefully evaluates the relative importance of various topics and prepares specifications outlining the educational outcomes to be measured. The questions are then written to correspond to the specifications. Content validity can be judged, in part, on the way in which the test was developed. It can also be judged on the basis of test descriptions and of an examination of the test itself. Although content validity is most directly relevant to achievement tests, it is also applicable to aptitude tests, provided that the person judging the content validity has a clear understanding of the kind of aptitudes the test is designed to measure.

Construct validity refers to the relationship between a measure and a hypothesis or construct, such as the construct of "motivation." It is a reasonable hypothesis that people who are highly motivated toward achievement will behave in various consistent ways: they will give up other opportunities in order to achieve the goal; they will apply themselves over long periods of time; they will forego pay, and so on. Each such form of behavior can be measured, sometimes by simple observation and sometimes by a test. If the scores on the tests and the observations are consistent in identifying the person who is believed to be motivated, each measure has gained a degree of validation by virtue of its logical "fit" with elements that could reasonably be expected to be related to it. If the measure confirms the hypothesis by behaving as if it were a measure of motivation, it is said to have construct validity.

The kind of validity that has been crucial to the widespread acceptance and use of standardized objective testing in college admissions is *predictive validity*, the usefulness of the test in the prediction of academic achievement at a future point in time, in this instance first year college or graduate school grades. This is expressed by a correlation coefficient and the higher the correlation, the more predictive the test.

In the field of testing for college admissions, substantial empirical research has been done. Proponents of aptitude testing expect the potential user to demand that the test predict success on a measure of performance chosen by the user. First year college grades are generally regarded by admissions officers and faculties as a reasonable measure of a student's success. These conditions set the stage for the proliferation of studies concerned with the effectiveness of aptitude tests for predicting college grades. The results of these studies differ in detail but have shown with remarkable consistency that both verbal and mathematical aptitude are relevant in the prediction of first year university grades. When high school grades are combined with test scores, the predictive validity is increased. In general, high school grades are the single best predictor of first year college performance.

One limitation of the validity coefficient as a measure of predictive effectiveness needs to be mentioned. If the coefficient is calculated for a group which has been selected in part on the basis of abilities measured by the predictors (high school grade point average and admissions tests scores), the coefficients will tend to be lower in the selected group than in the unselected group of applicants. Thus the correlation coefficients obtained in the selected group will tend to underestimate the predictive effectiveness which would be found if the entire applicant group could be studied. A consequence of this limitation is that universities whose students are relatively homogeneous in

verbal aptitude tend to have lower correlation coefficients
of predictors with first year college grades than universities
whose students are relatively heterogeneous in verbal aptitude.

A survey of 116 studies based on male freshmen and of
143 studies based on female freshmen in liberal arts programs yielded the following median correlations with
grades:

	Men	Women
Scholastic Aptitude Test—Verbal	.33	.41
Scholastic Aptitude Text—Mathematical	.30	.36
High school record	.47	.54
Three predictors combined	.55	.62

Some idea of the degree of relationship associated with different correlation coefficients of predictive validity can be
obtained by describing the probable standing on grades for
students in the top fifth on the predictor. The following
table shows results for various correlation coefficients:

Standing on university grades:	Percent of students in the top fifth on the predictor who would achieve various standings when correlation is:			
	.30	.40	.50	.60
Top fifth	33	38	44	50
Middle three-fifths	57	55	52	48
Bottom fifth	10	7	4	2

These figures make it clear that even when the correlation
is as low as .30, students in the top fifth on the predictor
are much more likely to appear in the top than in the bottom fifth when ranked by their university grades, and the
difference in performance increases as the correlation rises.
A high degree of predictive validity—as shown by a high
correlation coefficient—should not be the only factor

considered in making admissions decisions, however. As indicated on the table, even when the correlation is .60, 2 percent of students in the top fifth on the predictor would be expected to be in the bottom fifth on grades. Correlations which are found in prediction studies show that existing predictors will leave a great deal unexplained in terms of the individual's ability.

Although the correlations given above are an example of predictive validity, it is erroneous to assume that only one level of predictive validity exists for any test. Many colleges and graduate schools develop their own formulas and weight different factors according to their own experience and admissions philosophies. Despite this variation, test scores are clearly an important part of university admissions procedures because they provide a uniform measurement on which to judge all students, independent of teacher or school judgments.

The Use of Test Scores

In using objective aptitude tests or other kinds of tests, five major considerations should be kept in mind:

A test is only one indication of a student's ability or achievement.

Test scores, like all measures, are not perfectly precise and every test score, although reported as a specific number, should be considered as within a range of figures, the size of the range depending on a particular test.

Tests should normally only be used in the manner for which they are intended. The admissions tests discussed in this paper measure abilities and knowledge or skills that research has indicated contribute to success in study at a particular level or in a particular discipline. For example, a student's performance on the Law School Admission Test indicates—but not as the sole predictor—his or her ability to handle the work required during the first year in law school. It is not intended to indicate the student's ability to succeed in the practice of law or his or her ability to succeed in a graduate program in the arts and sciences. Tests are not measures of individual worth nor do they record innate ability. They measure *developed* skills.

Test scores should be interpreted within the limitations of their research-established reliability and validity. These limitations are indicated by the numerical coefficients discussed earlier. Even the highest correlations obtained leave a great deal unexplained.

In a heterogeneous population such as the United States, where certain groups have been hampered by poverty, racial discrimination, language barriers, and a history of unequal educational opportunity, the information provided by the test scores must be interpreted in the light of these factors. Although aptitude tests are not related closely to the curriculum, they do measure learned skills developed in school and elsewhere over a period of years. Consequently, students who have had less educational opportunity are likely to do less well on the tests and, at the same time, will have greater difficulty with programs which make use of these skills. If a college or graduate school makes an effort to help these students attain these skills, students from these groups can and do succeed. For this reason, the *College Board Guide for High Schools and Colleges,* a publication which discusses the use of SAT scores, contains the following information:

> Perhaps the best way to regard test scores for a student from a poor family—and that includes most, but not all, American Indians, Blacks, Chicanos, and Puerto Ricans—is as a floor under his abilities, but not as a ceiling... . Because of the debilitating effects of limited incomes and substandard schools in poor neighborhoods, a low-income student's test scores do not indicate how much he could have achieved—and may achieve later—under other circumstances.

Colleges and graduate schools in the United States tend to regard the scores of these students as recommended in the passage quoted and have instituted programs to assist them.

Institutional autonomy in all areas of U.S. postsecondary education is the prevailing rule in the United States. Generalizations about how test scores are used in the admissions process at both the undergraduate and graduate level are, therefore, difficult to make. Today the tests are less important for selection at the college level than previously because of the decreasing number of 18-year olds and the increasing number of options in education including open admissions. There is increasing use of the test in placement as indicated by the new section on the SAT-Verbal, which was instituted at the urging of college teachers of English. In contrast to the situation at the undergraduate level, the number of applicants for graduate study continues to rise, and the use of the test in selection at the graduate level continues to be important.

Among American colleges, high school grade point average (GPA) is the most important factor considered. As the earlier discussion of validity indicated, GPA is the best predictor of first year college performance. Similarly, at the graduate level, college grade point average is usually the most important single factor considered. However, admissions officers know that research has shown the objective admissions tests to be relevant for the prediction of first year performance and to be a uniform standard, and they use test scores in the admissions process. In addition to grade point average and test scores, admissions officers also consider recommendations, school and community activities, and evidence of motivation and creative ability.

Perhaps the most typical pattern in American universities which practice selective admissions at the undergraduate and graduate level is as follows: students with high grades and high test scores are accepted with less concern for other factors. Students with low grades and low test scores are likely to be rejected, unless some aspect of their total record suggests the need for further consideration.

The middle group—students with high grades and low scores, or low scores and high grades, or average grades and average scores—receives the greatest amount of time and consideration by admissions officers and committees. The relative importance of grades, scores, and other information may be different for different students and admissions staffs depending on a particular institution's pool of applicants and admissions philosophy. There is good reason to believe that few universities use a rigid cutoff score on test scores and grades as a basis for final decision.

Some Criticisms of the Objective Tests of Aptitude and Achievement Used in the U.S. College and Graduate Admissions Process

Because of their widespread acceptance, the college and graduate admissions tests in use in the United States have been subject to scrutiny and various kinds of criticisms.

1. *Aptitude tests reward mediocrity and conformity, not depth and measure rote recall.* Because objective tests touch on a relatively large number of topics in a given time period and because each question has a predetermined correct answer, this criticism identifies an important challenge to the test author. The author's task is to identify specific questions which permit a student who has a thorough understanding of the topic to demonstrate his insight. It is true that some students may be able to recognize the correct answer but would be unable to produce it on an essay test. On the other hand, the objective test requires the student to attempt the precise task which the examiner presents.

   Although some objective tests (and some essay tests) may measure rote recall, current objective tests used in large-scale testing programs carefully avoid this pitfall.

2. *Admissions tests create pressures for students and stand as barriers to their educational progress.* Under conditions which permit only a small percentage of applicants

to be accepted, *any* element which is considered important in the selection process could be seen as creating pressures or barriers. Because testing occurs at a time in the student's career when anxiety is likely to be high, the tests provide a highly visible target. The relatively short time required for the test is contrasted with the period of several years during which the student's aca- -demic record is accumulated. Research indicates that test performance is not affected by anxiety nor that it is markedly improved by a short, intensive period of coaching, although experience in taking objective tests is useful. The tests do enable the student to demonstrate how far he has developed the abilities measured by the test under conditions which are as uniform as possible for all students.

3. *Admissions tests rigidify the curriculum.* The validity of this criticism depends on how the tests are built. The criticism would apply with greatest force to achievement tests designed in terms of a narrowly defined, unchanging curriculum. Objective achievement tests of the kind used by the College Board can measure major outcomes which would be embodied in any sound curriculum. Because a large number of questions can be included, there is greater opportunity for different teaching emphases to balance out in the test as a whole. The test development process involves teachers of the subject in the preparation and review of questions and this increases the appropriateness of the final examination.

4. *Admissions tests serve universities not students.* This formulation implies both a substantial difference in interests between the student and the university and an admissions process which places sole or primary weight on the test scores. When test scores are considered in the exclusion of applicants who are very unlikely to be able to succeed in university programs, this criticism makes little sense. In the more selective universities, it is probably true that tests have contributed to an emphasis on academic promise in admissions. In this sense, they have

promoted a more open admissions policy than existed in
the past, a trend which is to the student's advantage as
well as the institution's. As stated earlier, colleges and
graduate schools consider other factors as well as test
scores in making admissions decisions. Finally, the test
provides the student with the opportunity to display his
or her ability on a measure common to all students and
uninfluenced by grading standards of a particular
teacher or school.

5. *Admissions tests are imperfect predictors.* It is indeed
true that some students perform much better in university work than their test scores and previous academic
record would predict and others perform much worse
than predicted. On the basis of this observation, some
critics have argued that the tests are worthless. This
argument is not supported by the research on performance. A variant of this criticism is that the existing
prediction is so weak as not to be worth making. Few
administrators with the responsibility for selecting applicants have found this argument persuasive. A third
group of critics have objected to the preoccupation with
predicting university grades and have urged that research
consider broader aspects of university success and of
success in life after the university. These critics are
making an important point. Far too little research using
broader and longer-range measures of success has been
done. In part, this unsatisfactory state of affairs is
attributable to the lack of agreed-upon indicators of success in college or success in life, and to the fact that research in this field is costly and difficult. Admissions
testing is, however, vulnerable to the criticism that too
little is known about the relationship of test scores to
college and career success.

6. *Admissions tests are culturally biased.* This topic has
long been a matter of concern in testing. In recent years,
special prominence has been given to cultural bias in the

efforts to ensure that minority group students are treated equitably in admissions. The argument that test scores are less effective in predicting university grades for minority group students than for white middle-class students is not supported by empirical research. This finding is not surprising in view of the fact that the tests are designed to measure the abilities needed for university work, which presumably would be the same for minority students as for others. Attempts to identify specific test questions which are relatively more difficult for minority or for white majority students have indicated that few such questions can be found in existing tests. It appears that aptitude tests are yielding a fair measure of the ability level of the student at the time of testing, since the tests measure skills developed over time through school and other experiences. To the extent that an educationally impoverished childhood impairs the development of the abilities measured by the tests, it can be argued that students having less favorable cultural backgrounds would be likely to perform less well on the test. In this sense, the tests may be culturally biased.

Standardized Tests and School-Leaving Examinations: Some Concluding Thoughts

A common set of school-leaving examinations as in Germany serves many of the functions of admissions tests such as the College Board's SAT in the United States, although Germany employs the essay and the United States the objective form. Most important, both examinations provide a single standard on which all students can demonstrate their ability, a standard not subject to individual school or teacher ratings.

For Germany, with a more uniform preparatory curriculum and a more homogeneous population than the United States, the development and use of standardized objective tests of aptitude and academic achievement are likely to provide less additional information than such measures do in the United States.

In the United States, local control over education has resulted in varied secondary school curricula and college preparation, and applicants represent a heterogeneous social, cultural, and economic population. The use of a standardized objective examination less tied to a specific curriculum is, therefore, quite important. Although the institution and use of objective tests of aptitude and academic achievement probably should be viewed as an addition rather than a substitution in access to German higher education, such tests might have advantages.

Aptitude tests of quantitative and verbal ability can provide additional information on a student's performance, information which is relatively free of the effects of specific cramming and of the excellence of immediately preceding instruction. Moreover, in the American experience, such tests have been shown to be useful in predicting future academic performance.

Objective tests of academic achievement, because they attain broader coverage than essay examinations, are more likely to be impartial—to provide students from various districts with the opportunity to perform well on the test. Objective tests would also remove the possibility of reader bias in favor of certain approaches or answers and have greater reliability. Finally, although they would require substantial research in the development process, objective tests could be more easily graded, a major concern in an expanding applicant population. Objective tests, however, may be less successful at measuring highly developed skills, and parents and teachers may raise this issue. This issue is less important when scores constitute only one factor in making decisions.

As in any decision regarding use of a test, before final evaluation of the usefulness of objective college admissions tests for German higher education is made, research should be undertaken on the reliability of the objective tests and on the contribution which scores achieved on these tests can make to the prediction of university performance.

NONINTELLECTUAL FACTORS IN ADMISSIONS

Simon V. Keochakian
University of Massachusetts

NONINTELLECTUAL
FACTORS IN
ADMISSIONS

A review of the literature on college admissions is a sobering experience because of the realization that this is anything but a scientific endeavor. College admissions staffs in the United States have been going about their work for decades (in some cases centuries) using procedures which are indefensible and have little or no supporting evidence. Coupled with this troublesome situation is the fact that no systematic, comprehensive research program has ever been implemented which would attempt to remedy the problem.

Unfortunately, admissions personnel have expressed little interest in studying their own professional work and relatively few have the necessary training or expertise to mount a program of research. The little research that has been done on admissions is often performed by individuals or teams from the behavioral sciences, typically psychology, who do so as part of their work for a research grant. This area has also proved to be a popular area for doctoral dissertations in psychology and education.

However, much of the work that has been done deals with the relationship of academic and intellectual factors to various measures of success in college or university studies. While there has been a proliferation of such studies, available evidence suggests that researchers may have reached a ceiling with regard to such a relationship. Gough (1967) points out these relationship studies done in various medical schools seldom report correlations which exceed +.25 to +.30. [A correlation (r) is a statistical measure of relationship which has a theoretical range of -1.0 to +1.0.] While such correlations usually achieve statistical significance, they have little value as predictive indicators. (An estimate of common variance accounted for by the correlation is r^2.) Thus, a correlation of +.30 accounts for only 9 percent of the common variance of that relationship. In some unusual instances, correlations of +.50 between an academic predictor and university performance are reported. But even in these situations, 75 percent of the variance remains unaccounted for! On the basis of available evidence it appears that academic and/or intellectual predictors are unlikely to add little additional predictive power to admissions procedures.

If the foregoing assessment of the admissions situation is accurate, then we must examine nonintellectual factors in an attempt to elevate the efficacy of selection procedures. While this particular process is by itself a complex problem, one needs to ask, in addition, whether existing practitioners are effective role models. Taking an optimistic position, one may assume that additional study will produce a procedure which will be highly valid and provide admissions staffs with useful tools. However, are we justified in developing efficient procedures which will only insure that future professionals and practitioners are exact duplicates of present practitioners?

Such a philosophical question is, in some respects, beyond the scope of this paper, but educators must be constantly mindful of that issue if the university is to reduce its elitist influence. To ignore this issue will only serve to compound problems of the past.

As the title suggests, this paper focuses on a review of the literature pertaining to the role of nonintellectual factors in admission to higher education, especially graduate and professional education. Specifically, an attempt is made to report on the actual or potential role that personality factors, biographical data, and interview information can play in the admissions process. While available data on these topics are limited and somewhat inconclusive, there are a sufficient number of encouraging and suggestive reports to warrant a close examination of this area. Interestingly, much of the available information regarding personality correlates of educational and professional success is based on work with physicians. In contrast, relatively little substantive research regarding the selection interview has been done in an academic setting. Instead, it is necessary to look at work done in an industrial setting in order to get some insights into the functioning of the selection interview process. Fortunately, three excellent reviews on this topic are available (Mayfield, 1964; Ulrich and Trumbo, 1965; and Wright, 1969).

Personality and Related Studies

Unfortunately, the absence of a systematic research program in university admissions creates a severe problem in terms of evaluating and relating findings from discrete research projects. This results in a vast unrelated array of both predictor and criterion variables. In addition, criterion variables are drawn both from academic and clinical performance as well as professional performance subsequent to formal education programs. To make the situation even more confusing, various predictor variables which are found to be related to university performance have little or no relationship to professional performance. For example, various studies have demonstrated that undergraduate grade point average (GPA) and scores on the Medical College Admission Test (MCAT) are significantly related to performance in medical school. However, the overwhelming weight of the evidence indicates that no such relationship exists in terms of physician performance.

Howell (1966) reported a study with physicians in the U.S. Public Health Service in which she compared individuals with highly favorable ratings by superiors with individuals with clearly unfavorable ratings. On three of the MCAT subtests, the scores were in favor of the physicians with unfavorable ratings. Essentially, the study indicated that there were no intellectual measures available which would differentiate between the two groups.

Price, Taylor, Richards and Jacobsen (1964) did a rather extensive study with a broad cross-section of physicians (full-time medical faculty members, board-qualified specialists, urban general practitioners, and rural general practitioners) in an attempt to study the relationship between academic predictors and on-the-job performance. Of the 849 intercorrelations computed, 97 percent were of a zero-order magnitude. With this large number of intercorrelations, one can expect at least 3 percent of them to be significant on the basis of chance alone.

Based on these findings, Dr. Price made the following comments:

> This is a somewhat shocking finding for a medical educator like myself who has spent his professional life selecting applicants for admission to medical school, and in teaching and grading students after admission. It is true that a strong suspicion that grades have been weighted much too heavily in predicting performance in medical school and after graduation from medical school is what led to the initiation of this whole study in the first instance; but to have that suspicion so forcefully corroborated has led me to question the adequacy of some of our traditional admission policies, as well as the reliability of conventional grades as a measure of progress of the student during his medical course . . . (p. 209).

In a similar vein, Coppedge (1969) found that various high school predictor variables (GPA, academic tests, and teacher ratings of personal attributes) proved to be related to college performance, but showed no relationship to occupational success of those not going on to college. This was true for both academic and nonacademic predictors.

The existing data thus suggest that academic and intellectual predictors, while statistically related to university performance, have limited value in terms of predictive power. In addition, these same academic predictors seem to be essentially unrelated to occupational success. However, the admissions picture is not completely hopeless since various researchers have found that certain nonintellectual factors are related both to university performance and occupational success.

Howell (1966), in the study referred to previously, found that numerous personality variables did discriminate between two groups of U.S. Public Health Service physicians (one with strongly favorable ratings by supervisors and the other with unfavorable ratings) even though more traditional academic predictors did not do so. She points out that the personally effective physician is ". . . characterized by greater social presence, sense of well-being, socialization, maturity and responsibility, flexibility, achievement potential, and intellectual efficiency . . . More than his low counterpart . . . , he tends to be serious, sober, responsive to obligations, diligent, loyal, helpful, self-disciplined, conventional, solicitous, adaptable, concerned with position, moderate, hesitant to take the initiative, conforming but not lacking in courage, sincere, conscientious, dependable, persevering, and self-denying" (p. 457).

The kind of person that Howell has described is a rather compliant, unexciting, efficient but probably unimaginative, and sociable individual. This type of individual fits nicely into the organizational structure and is unlikely to be a dissident force leading to change. Interestingly, this rather conservative tendency is also reported by other researchers. It will be discussed later.

Gough (1967) reported a project which studied accepted and rejected applicants to medical school. In this instance he found significant differences in personality attributes between applicants favored by interviewers and those who received an unfavorable rating by these same interviewers. He summarizes his findings with these comments: ". . . the normal, sensible, well-organized, and tactful applicant is favored, whereas the nervous, individualistic, and perhaps skeptical applicant is not" (pp. 647-648).

Gough and Hall (1964), in a study of the personality characteristics of successful performers in medical school, found that the influence which operates at the admission phase of medical study continues through medical training. Those individuals who adapt, fit in and do not alienate others tend to be the ones who are evaluated by medical school faculty as being the successful student.

Gough (1967) summarizes these findings rather forcefully:

> . . . from the personality standpoint, all of the forces that guide an individual toward selection of medicine as a career, toward gaining entry into the training program, toward doing well in this program, and toward performing in professional practice in a way that will be recognized and rewarded tend to converge on a greater and greater conformity to a kind of civilized, considerate, well-socialized, functionally efficient, and sensible role-model.

> If there were only one kind of man who could practice medicine and contribute to the profession in a responsible and commendable way, one could hardly do better than to choose rationally what current methods of selection and training appear to produce naturally . . . (p. 649).

Biographical Studies

While the use of personality tests has offered one productive process to study nonintellectual factors in university admissions, it is by no means the only approach available. The next area of discussion, the biographical approach, may prove to be of even more value once it is refined to the same degree that psychological testing has evolved. It has the additional value of being less intrusive and less objectionable than the personality testing approach.

Unfortunately, there has been no coordination of the various attempts to study biographical factors, and the result has been a very disjointed and noncomplementary approach to the problem. During a six-year period (1968-1974), four important studies in this area were reported in the literature, but the authors seemed to have little or no awareness of the work of the others.

Korman, Stubblefield, and Martin (1968) used the biographical approach as well as personality tests, interview data, and academic information in an attempt to determine the correlates of patterns of success in medical school. While their results were rather modest and nondiscriminating, they did provide a systematic method of defining success in medical education. Using the factor analysis method, they were able to reduce a tremendous quantity of data to five factors. These factors are labeled as follows: ". . . (a) General Achievement in Clinical Medicine (ACM)—total GPA, third-year GPA, fourth-year GPA; (b) Internship Success (IS)—components of the intership rating scale exclusively; (c) Peer Esteem—suitable as partner, skilled in patient relationship; (d) Scientist Potential—likely to accept salaried position, suitable as researcher and teacher, interested in diagnosis versus treatment; and (e) Humanism (H)—interested in public health, suitable as a general practitioner, internship rating of integrity high (pp. 405-406)."

While Korman, et al. (1968) spent considerable effort in refining their criterion variables, they neglected to do so with their predictor variables. Their discouraging results may have been due in part to this lack of refinement.

Worthington and Grant (1971) utilized a number of pre-college demographic and biographical characteristics to study factors affecting first-quarter grades of a diverse sample of undergraduate students. The results indicated that numerous nonintellectual and nonacademic variables are significantly correlated with first quarter grades. Since the research design involved a multivariate analysis, it was possible to examine the interdependence of two or more predictor variables as related to the criterion variable (grades). Significant interaction of some of the predictor variables was found, indicating that these variables were differentially related to the criterion, depending on the value of its paired predictor variable.

This latter point is probably the most important aspect of the Worthington and Grant (1971) study since it points out empirically that the study of admission criteria is a complex matter. Many of the studies in this area have utilized the simple Pearson product-moment correlation as the analysis method. However, this permits only a simple comparison of one predictor with one criterion. Consequently, a more subtle co-variation of two predictor variables relative to the criterion would not be discovered. Some of the nonsignificance reported in the literature may be due to the fact that the analysis techniques have not been sufficiently powerful to identify the existing relationships.

Perhaps the most significant contribution to the study of biographical factors in relation to university success and career performance is the work of Loughmiller, Ellison, Taylor, and Price (1973). These researchers, studying a sample of 333 physicians, have dealt with both the issue of defining what constitutes a "good" career practitioner (the criterion problem) and the predictor problem of assessing in advance which applicants are most likely to become these "good" career practitioners and not just good students. The technique used in this study is referred to as the

Biographical Inventory (BI) approach. The medical BI used was developed by Jacobsen, Price, deMik, and Taylor (1965) and represents the final product of an elaborate process for reducing over 1,000 original biographical items to the 351-item final form. "The BI sought information concerning four major periods in each physicians life, including: (1) home life and early schooling, (2) college life and experiences, (3) professional education and training, and (4) adult life and vocation" (Loughmiller et al. 1973, p. 271).

This study utilized ten criteria variables, developed from a broad range of success measures. Some of these are as follows: (a) a composite value based on such things as number of times nominated as preferred consultant, gross income from medical profession, number of refresher courses taken during career, number of patients seen per day, self-estimated value of office equipment, etc.; (b) a rating of history and accomplishments of each physician by several expert judges; (c) self-report of contributions to the medical profession, science, and society evaluated by expert physician judges; (d) ratings of colleagues by a number of widely knowledgeable and distinguished physician judges; and (e) various indicators of specialization level and academic criteria.

While the study by Loughmiller et al. (1973) produced several interesting findings, two of the results are particularly pertinent to this report. First, this project resulted in considerable refinement of the Biographical Inventory technique and this should be particularly useful to future researchers. More important, many of the empirically derived BI scoring keys were highly significantly correlated to their respective criterion variables. Interesting, the keys derived to predict GPA resulted in the lowest correlations with their respective criterion variables. Of the keys derived to predict the ten criterion measures, one reached +.56 and four ranged from +.40 to +.48. Such results, while providing limited predictive power, are very encouraging at this very early stage of development of the BI procedure.

The fourth study in this cluster (Richards, Calkins, McCanse, and Burgess, 1974) was designed to investigate the prediction of success in the six-year combined undergraduate and medical education program at the University of Missouri—Kansas City. This is a rather unique program where students enter this program directly from high school. In addition to the usual measures of academic success, criteria for this study included measures of personal development, participation in cultural and community activities, and attitudes and plans with respect to various kinds of medical careers. The 50 predictor variables included: previous academic performance; tests of ability, vocational interests, and personality; overall evaluation by two interviewers, one a clinician and the other a nonclinician; measures of personal development and participation in cultural and community activities; and attitudes and plans with respect to various kinds of medical careers.

While the study utilized a rather sophisticated analysis procedure, the stepwise multiple correlation approach, no attempt was made to refine either the predictor or criterion variables. Instead, the study utilized a rather indiscriminate approach of trying to relate every predictor to each of the criteria. The general findings are hardly surprising. Richards et al. (1974) report that: "The best predictor for any given criterion variable tended to be previous standing on that variable. In general, adding other variables improved prediction only a little, and the variables that were added often had little rational relationship to the specific criterion in question" (pp. 926-927). The authors went on to point out that measures of personality and vocational interest made little contribution to the prediction of most criteria.

The practical value of the study by Richards et al. (1974) is difficult to assess. While they report several multiple correlations in excess of .60, most of these have meaning only for the program at the University of Missouri–Kansas City and have little applicability to more traditional programs. However, the study demonstrates that biographical and background data must be considered seriously if the prediction of university success is to be enhanced. In addition, the work done points out rather clearly that sophisticated statistical techniques are effective tools, but they cannot be substituted for the necessary difficult phase of refining both predictor and criterion variables.

Summary of Interview Research

Perhaps the single statement that will most clearly describe the selection interview is that it is widely used (perhaps overused) and grossly misunderstood. Admissions staffs, personnel managers, and anyone else who is in a position to make selection decisions have been involved in interview activities in some form or another. Very likely, each of these individuals claims that the interview is a very critical and useful part of the decision-making process. However, such a claim would be in direct contradiction to the available research, of which there are literally hundreds of studies.

The use of the selection interview in academic institutions, while still extensive, is on the decline because of the press of numbers arising from mass education. Yet the incidence of current use is not insignificant, and the interview is still widely used in many professional schools. However, academicians are as guilty as individuals in the business and industrial world in terms of utilizing a procedure which is of unproven validity. One might expect that academicians would be more inclined to study the interview process because of the learned and scientific environment in which they work. Instead, the opposite is true. A rather significant portion of the available research has been done in a business setting with the intent of finding a better procedure to select employees for specific jobs. Thus, much of the literature surrounding this topic comes from business sources, but selection for a job and selection for professional school are not particularly dissimilar. Principles of selection interviewing drawn from one area should be applicable to the other.

A thorough review of the literature on the selection interview would be impossible within the limits of this paper. Such a procedure is quite unnecessary since three excellent reviews (Mayfield, 1964; Ulrich and Trumbo, 1965; and Wright, 1969) are available for us to examine. Unfortunately, there have been no significant new contributions in the past six years which would change the situation since the report by Wright (1969). One further article will be reviewed because of its pertinence to the field of medical education. This is the work of Burgess, Calkins, and Richards (1972).

Mayfield (1964) has categorized his findings under 15 major topics, summarized below:

1. The interview can be divided into various types of units, and this can be done reliably.

2. The intrarater reliability of the interview appears to be satisfactory.

3. An interviewer is consistent in his approach to different interviewees; the techniques he uses remain fairly constant.

4. A general suitability rating based on an unstructured interview with no prior information provided has extremely low interrater reliability.

5. In an unstructured interview, material is not consistently covered.

6. When interviewers obtain the same information, they are likely to interpret or weight it differently.

7. Structured interviews, in general, provide a higher interrater reliability than do unstructured interviews.

8. Although the reliabilities of interviews may be high in given situations, the validities obtained are usually of a low magnitude.

9. When an individual interviewer has tests of proven validity available, his predictions based on the interview and the test scores are no more (and frequently less) accurate than those based on test scores alone.

10. With respect to traits or characteristics which can be estimated reliably and validly from interviews, it seems that only the intelligence or mental ability of the interviewee can be judged satisfactorily.

11. The form of the question does affect the answer obtained.

12. The attitudes of interviewers do affect their interpretation of what the interviewee says.

13. In the usual unstructured employment interview, the interviewer talks more than does the interviewee.

14. Interviewers appear to be influenced more by unfavorable than favorable information.

15. Interviewers tend to make their decision early in an unstructured interview.

Although Ulrich and Trumbo (1965) published their article shortly after Mayfield (1964) and attempted to review essentially the same material, there was only about a 25 percent overlap in the articles included in the respective reviews. Yet the findings in the two reviews were not particularly dissimilar. Both found that the research done was quite uncoordinated and very unsystematic, thus making comparisons across studies very difficult if not impossible. While many of the conclusions of Ulrich and Trumbo (1965) were similar to those of Mayfield (1964), there were a few noteworthy additional findings. They noted two additional areas in which validity studies have proved fruitful: the determination of motivation to work and personal relations. Personal relations essentially deals with the applicant's ability to adjust to the social context of his job. The findings perhaps suggest that the interview should be limited in scope rather than trying to cover too many topics.

While Wright (1969) reviewed 53 articles published since 1964, his findings add very little of practical value to the individual who wants to enhance the efficacy of his interviewing. However, some of his points should be considered. He notes: "The consistent finding that independent judges can assess interviewee behavior as validly and as accurately as the participant interviewer has important implications for future research in the employment interview, since it further substantiates the suggestion that interview decisions are made on the basis of behavioral as well as verbal cues . . . Undoubtedly, interviewer skill is directly related to the validity, quantity and quality of output" (pp. 407-408). Wright (1969) also points out that the literature on small group behavior should be investigated for possible insights into the decision-making process as it occurs in the board interview where several interviewers judge the same candidate at the same time. In a related area, the leaderless group discussion technique was found to be equally as valid and reliable as the individual interview approach in terms of a selection decision.

The final study to be reviewed in this paper is the work of Burgess, Calkins, and Richards (1972) which was a project designed to evaluate the structured interview in the selection of students for a six-year joint bachelor's-medical degree program at the University of Missouri—Kansas City. Each candidate was interviewed by both a physician and a nonphysician, using the structured interview format. Each interviewer rated each interviewee on several traits plus making an overall recommended admissions decision.

The general results were not particularly encouraging and tend to confirm the negative results of other studies.

The findings of Burgess et al. (1972) are as follows: (a) except for the overall decision as to whether to accept or reject an applicant, the extent of agreement between physicians and nonphysicians was low; (b) both interviewers tended to form their opinions on the basis of an overall global impression of the applicant rather than on the basis of the applicant's individual personal characteristics; (c) the correlations between physician and nonphysician ratings were low; and (d) the influence of both the physician and nonphysician interviewers' recommendations on the Selection Council's decision was relatively low.

While this study did shed some light on the role of the structured interview in the medical school selection process, as the authors indicated, the net practical gain was very little. Much more research needs to be done before the selection interview can be embraced as a useful tool in the admissions process.

Conclusions

By far the most significant conclusion that can be drawn from this report is the fact that university admissions (and prediction) is a highly complex phenomenon. Unfortunately, most researchers have not been particularly mindful of this fact and have attempted to wrestle with the complexity by using simplistic procedures. The evidence points out quite clearly that gross measures are inappropriate and further work of this sort should be avoided. In addition, the uncoordinated and individualistic approach used in attempting to cope with an issue which should be of national concern is unlikely to produce a very fruitful resolution to the present problem.

There seems to be some indication that attempts to attack this issue on a global basis are also likely to be unproductive. Instead, each discipline must be analyzed and studied to determine factors of success and achievement *in that particular discipline*. More work should be done to study occupational "success" rather than "success" in training programs since the factors which lead to favorable ratings in the latter may be quite unrelated to the former. Personality and biographical variables appear to offer some promise in terms of studying rated occupational "success," but various researchers (and this author) seem inclined to raise the question whether a refinement of selection procedures which will solidify the existing professional structure will serve the greater good of society. Finally, the U.S. approach to university admissions must be recognized as being burdened with serious limitations, and an attempt to copy anything other than selected aspects would be an invitation to receive justifiable criticism.

REFERENCES

Burgess, M.M., V. Calkins and J.M. Richards, "The Structured Interview: A Selection Device," *Psychological Reports.* 1972, 31, 867-877.

Carlson, R.E., "Selection Interview Decisions: The Relative Influence of Appearance and Factual Written Information on an Interviewer's Final Rating," *Journal of Applied Psychology.* 1967, 51, 461-468.

Coppedge, F.L., "Relation of Selected Variables from High School Records to Occupational and College Success," *Journal of Education Research.* 1969, 63, 71-73.

Gough, H.G., "Nonintellectual Factors in the Selection and Evaluation of Medical Students," *Journal of Medical Education,* 1967, 42, 642-650.

Gough, H.G., and W.B. Hall, "Prediction of Performance in Medical School from the California Psychological Inventory," *Journal of Applied Psychology.* 1964, 48, 218-226.

Hamilton, V., "Scholastic and Non-Scholastic Correlates of University Students' Academic Performance," *Research into Higher Education.* Papers presented at the 4th Annual Conference, 1968. London.

Hobson, P., "The Effects of a Personal Interview on Student Admission," *British Dental Journal.* 1974, 137, 181-184.

Howell, M.A., "Personal Effectiveness of Physicians in a Federal Health Organization," *Journal of Applied Psychology.* 1966, 50, 451-459.

Jabobsen, T.L., P.B. Price, B. deMik and C.W. Taylor, *An exploratory study of predictors of physicians performance.* U.S. Office of Education, Contract No. CE-3-10-136, 1965.

Korman, M., R.L. Stubblefield and L.W. Martin, "Patterns of Success in Medical School and Their Correlates," *Journal of Medical Education.* 1968, 43, 405-411.

Loughmiller, G.C., R.L. Ellison, C.W. Taylor and P.B. Price, "Predicting Career Performance of Physicians Using the Biographical Inventory Approach," *Journal of Vocational Behavior.* 1973, 3, 269-278.

Mayfield, E.C., "The Selection Interview—A Re-evaluation of Published Research," *Personnel Psychology.* 1964, 17, 239-260.

Price, P.B., C.W. Taylor, J.M. Richards, Jr. and T.L. Jacobsen, "Measurement of Physician Performance," *Journal of Medical Education.* 1964, 39, 203-211.

Richards, J.M., Jr., E.V. Calkins, E.V. McCanse and M.M. Burgess, "Predicting Performance in a Combined Undergraduate and Medical Education Program," *Educational and Psychological Measurement.* 1974, 34, 923-931.

Taylor, C.W. and R.L. Ellison, "Biographical Predictors of Scientific Performance," *Science,* 1967, 155, 1075-1080.

Ulrich, L., and D. Trumbo, "The Selection Interview Since 1949," *Psychological Bulletin.* 1965, 63, 100-116.

Worthington, L.H., and C.W. Grant, "Factors at Academic Success: A Multivariate Analysis," *Journal of Educational Research.* 1971, 65, 7-10.

Wright, O.R., Jr., "Summary of Research on the Selection Interview Since 1964," *Personnel Psychology.* 1969, 22, 391-413.

APPENDIX

Study Group Membership

James A. Perkins, Study Group Chairman
Chairman, International Council for Educational Development.

Barbara B. Burn, Study Group Director ,
Director, International Programs, University of Massachusetts, Amherst.

Horst Bahro, Pädagogische Hochschule Rheinland, Cologne.

Willi Becker
Director General, Ministry for Higher Education and Research, North Rhine Westfalia, Düsseldorf.

Eberhard Böning
Director General for Higher Education, Federal Ministry for Education and Science, Germany.

John Z. Bowers, M.D.
President, Josiah Macy, Jr. Foundation.

Frank Bowles (deceased 1975)
Consultant, International Council for Educational Development.

Ladislav Cerych
Director, Institute of Education, European Cultural Foundation.

Mrs. Gertrude Hasemann
German Study Group Coordinator.

Karl G. Hasemann (deceased 1975)
  Secretary-General, Federal-State Commission for Educational Planning.
Clark Kerr
  Chairman, Carnegie Council on Policy Studies in Higher Education.
Hans Leussink, Karlsruhe University.
Larry G. Simon
  Law Center, University of Southern California.
William W. Turnbull
  President, Educational Testing Service.

Publications of the German-U.S. Study Group on Access to Higher Education

Recent Student Flows in Higher Education. Ignace Hecquet, Christiane Verniers, and Ladislav Cerych, 1976. $2.50

Barriers to Higher Education in the Federal Republic of Germany. Willi Becker, 1977 (written in 1976). $2.00

Admission to Medical Education in Ten Countries. Barbara B. Burn, editor, 1978. $6.00

Admission to Higher Education in the United States: A German Critique. Ulrich Teichler, 1978. $5.00

Innovation in Access to Higher Education: Ontario, Canada; England and Wales; and Sweden. Robert M. Pike, Naomi E.S. McIntosh, and Urban Dahlöf, 1978. $10.00

Access Policy and Procedure and the Law in U.S. Higher Education. Larry G. Simon, Alice J. Irby, Jenne K. Britell and William B. Schrader, and Simon V. Keochakian, 1978. $6.00

Access to Higher Education: Two Perspectives. A Comparative Study of the Federal Republic of Germany and the United States of America. Final Report of the German-U.S. Study Group, 1978. $2.50